Testimonials

Subscriber Emails Received After the October–November 2008 Market Melt-Down

I have been trading the equity markets with many different strategies for over 40 years. Terry Allen's strategies have been the most consistent money makers for me. I used them during the 2008 melt-down, to earn over 50% annualized return, while all my neighbors were crying about their losses.

— JOHN COLLINS

I wonder if you remember when I boasted to you that I was switching my wife's IRA from American Century Fund to an options account using your strategy, and that I would turn her $65,000 into 100K within a year? This morning her IRA is $103,800. If it was still in AmCentury it would be about $45,000. The spreads were always invested in SPY very similar to your original strategy/or similar to your current "Big Dripper" portfolio.

My traditional, CONSERVATIVE, retirement rollover IRA/Pension accumulated over 30 yrs with 40% bonds and 60% stocks is down by 36% over the same period of time, while all seven of my option portfolios have a gain of some kind.

— FRED RYLAND

Terry's Tips is an ongoing educational experience for me. The Mesa approach offers the opportunity to view the changes in the market, the effects of extreme price swings, volatility and theta and still realize a profit! This trading reality has been more valuable to me than any text. The Saturday reports are a valuable adjunct, giving a detailed view of each portfolio, analyzing the past week's performance and projecting "what-if's" for the next week/expiration month.

Many thanks to Terry and his staff!

— EMORSINI

D0173386

. . . . an extremely Profitable first half of 2008, then, *Armageddon* hit in the Fall, Summary Of my results: My personal Option Strategy accts lost 98.8 %, My *Terrys Tips* Might Mesa Account GAINED 34 % . . . Incredible!

— MARK OTT

It is often said that options are to stock trading as chess is to checkers. I was looking to find the chess master amongst the checker's champs, and Terry is the one. Looking for the very smart yet understandable way to trade options? Look no further.

— PHIL WELLS

Terry's Tips makes me feel smarter than the professionals by out performing the market even during the worst down-turn in decades!

— GAVILÁN

As a result of your new Big Dripper portfolio, I've been able to make substantial gains. To date, the annualized rate of return has been just under 70%. More importantly, the wide profit range of SPY prices makes it quite suitable for the current volatile environment.

— MARK CHAPMAN

Bravo for Terry! Over the past months while the markets in general have tanked and had historically high volatility, Terry's strategies have managed to show impressive gains. He has developed a method for making profits with options, even when the markets are gyrating in huge ranges and the typical investor is experiencing painful losses.

— MARY ANN NORFLEET, PhD

Just in case nobody is praising you, let me do just that! I am fascinated that I have made money both in an up market and in a down market — with no additional trades. Maybe someday I can figure out how you do it, but I love autotrade, so I had rather let you do it and I will play golf. You are doing great!!! KEEP IT UP! PLEASE!

— LARRY WOODMAN

Earlier praise for the 2008 Edition of **Making 36%**
and **Terry's Tips**
(the option newsletter that carries out the **Mighty Mesa Strategy***)*

I would like to express my satisfaction with following: I began the year with approximately $80K and thus far (December 3, 2007) I have just over $150K gross (before commissions). That represents about 87% growth. I did not have all these strategies in place from the beginning of the year, but I calculate that if I did, I could have well broken the century mark in growth percentage. This performance far surpasses anything I've ever done in stocks, mutual funds and (don't remind me), investment real estate. I'm definitely planning to increase my capital allocation for 2008. I also thank you for your recommendation of thinkorswim. They are a first rate outfit.

— Brad Dunn

After 40 years of searching for the ideal strategy for a small investor, I'm so glad I found you. My Saturday mornings are spent eagerly awaiting your weekly report. Your strategy is near perfection for extremely good returns and manageable risk.

— Wayne Wolf, CPA

I have been a subscriber to *Terry's Tips* for almost a year. This is a unique service which includes a once-a-week commentary on how the various portfolios are doing. This is an honest commentary unlike most services which try to cover their failings with phony numbers. Terry actually discusses failures as well as successes. I am happy to report that there are many more successes than failures. I have read many books on option trading and can honestly say that I have learned more from Terry's almost off-hand teaching than all of the books.

— Jim Needham

I love your program, and have been trading it for just over a year now. I also want to thank you for my new BMW 5 series. I promised myself, (and convinced my wife) that I would buy it once I doubled my initial investment through using your program. I did it, and my new car is now on order.

— Joe P.

I was a subscriber back in the rough times we had trading back in 2004. I came back on board about 4 months ago and I have already made back 75% of what was lost back in 2004 in a full year's trading. I'm extremely glad I made the decision to come back.

— Tom La Bissoniere

I have been a subscriber of *Terry's Tips* for the past 5 months. Everyone should try his initial offer and get a feel for his service, web site and study the results. The service has been everything the site advertises. Terry's Tips service has exceeded all my expectations. He offers a very good service and speaking for my results, he has over-delivered.

— Tom Stidham

At 55 years old, I've been "playing" with the stock market for years, mostly with very limited success. The majority of my life savings is in multiple mutual funds which, as we all know, are considered superior if they (inconsistently) have returns of 10–11%. After less than six months of investing some IRA funds into two *Terry's Tips* portfolios, however, you've caused me to believe that I really will be able to retire on a nice income — and, hopefully, in the not too distant future. Thanks for the spectacular returns and thanks for being willing to share your knowledge and insights.

— Cliff Frish

Those who like to use the cliché that if it's too good to be true, it probably is, surely don't know about *Terry's Tips* and the 36% Solution! Being retired, I very much appreciate the concept of a monthly income generator that the 36% Solution has proven to be. Thanks for a little book that changed my life's perspective.

— Stanley E. Cesel, DVM

I can't figure out why everyone isn't using calendar spreads using your method. Sometimes it seems too good to be true. My returns the past two years have been almost unbelievable. I don't even try to tell anyone about it because they wouldn't believe me.

— Fred R.

After 25+ years at this, I have seen a lot of experts come and go. I have only found two where I consistently make money by following their experience and methods; one that I have followed since the 80s in the Hogs and Bellies at the Chicago Merc, and you. Nice work!

— BOB DUPRE

. . . . with the market at its current lower level, that in the past it would take months and some times years to recover with stocks and mutual funds, whereas the spreads that I have using your system take a couple of weeks to recover with far less upward movement in the market. I know that with my holdings in stocks and mutual funds in the past that the most recent decline would look pretty bad on my statements. Right now, I'm way ahead of my July holdings from the market peak over 14,000. I've pulled out $25,000 to remodel my house and I'm still $50,000 up in my account after the withdrawals.

— MARC PARKER

I autotrade in 2 different accounts, all your strategies. I read everything you write on Saturdays. I love your happiness thoughts and everything else. I usually do not communicate at all but I had to tell you how well my accounts with you are doing compared to everything else. You are awesome. Keep up the good work.

— MAYA JAGSIA

I don't know if a lot of subscribers thank you but my wife and I have watched the money that we have invested in your program grow at an alarming rate. We especially like the fact, which no other investments offer, the ability to cash out profits every month if they are earned. Cheers to you and your staff.

— ROB SLAVING

Just wanted to keep you informed of what I am doing in OIH. My profits to date are $18,322 (in 7 months) on a $34K investment using your strategy.

— ROGER ADAMS

I have confidence in your system . . . I have seen it work very well . . .
currently I have had a first 100% gain, and am now working to diversify
into more portfolios. This kind of trading is actually an "art"... I have my
own field of expertise...but sadly I can only offer my great appreciation to
what you do so instinctively.

— JAY GIALLOMBARDO

I started with your service about 7 months ago using three different
portfolios worth $70k. Those changed of course over time, but today I am
using 5 of the portfolios and the value just crossed the $100k mark (actual-
ly $101k) this morning. I consider this quite remarkable considering I have
been investing for the last 25 years and have never seen consistent gains as
you have shown me.

— MARK BAILEY

I have a PhD in math, but make my living from computers (software). It
is fair to say that during the last 25+ years I spent THOUSANDS of hours
reading, learning, simulating and developing trading systems. Since I sub-
scribed to your service, I spend most of my research time on it and I gain
bigger and bigger confidence that "this is it" (for me). I learn something
new from every single report. It is extremely useful for me that you don't
simply list the changes to be made, but reveal the thought process behind
them and discuss alternatives. I feel that these lessons will make me a better
trader.

— JOSEPH J.

I am fascinated Terry's philosophy and technique. After having suffered
through several booms and many more busts with my modest, self-manage
brokerage account, it's a true pleasure to be able to be invested in a vehicle
that's not so directly tied to the fortunes of a single company. And while
I could probably achieve this same ease-of-mind with a mutual or index
fund, I would have to be happy with a far more modest gain than what I've
experienced with Terry.

— EUGENE HILL

I am very very pleased with the performance of the portfolios. I've been interested in options for a very long time, but this seems to work more of the time and with better results. So I just keep moving more and more money from my self directed Ameritrade account to the autotrade accounts at thinkorswim.

— JUSTIN WODDIS

I thought you might appreciate some kind words from a devoted follower of your strategy far across the Atlantic in Germany. Even though the markets have been a little bit choppy due to subprime issues and wild volatility, you continue to make money for me beyond my wildest expectations. I can only thank you for being there for me and turning my investment world into a new and rewarding experience.

As a side note, I have to admit that I have in the past spent a lot of money and time being tutored on trading options. None of these courses came close to explaining how to manipulate and adjust the given strategy as you have so expertly done in your tutorial literature. What I liked about your approach is that you've managed to explain your strategy in terms that the layman can understand.

— PHIL DAVIS

Am I satisfied with *Terry's Tips*? — YES, YES, YES. I'm retired so I have the time to do my own trading and I enjoy trading. When the email notices arrive I always try to get a better price — sometimes I do and sometimes I don't. The reason for doing the trades is easy to understand, the trades are easy to do and best of all, it's profitable. Who could ask for more?

— LINSA NELSON

After 47 years of being very active in the market, I feel as though we found the Holy Grail. Also, I can't tell you how happy I am with Kurt at thinkorswim. He has been most helpful and a delight to work with.

— PETER J. KUEHN

My portfolio had incurred many losses until I adopted Terry's strategies. (Two other investment newsletters) consistently lost money trading options (by betting on a positive or negative direction for the underlying). The Dr's strategy is the only one I have seen or tested myself that consistently produces profits, not the "hit it out of the park" profits that so many newsletter authors and advisors claim, but market beating profits that you can count on.

— TOMMY HIETT

I want to take some time to personally thank you. Not only thanks to you the money that I am investing is growing five times faster than before, but I have also spurred me to get informed, and I have learned a lot. I am actually finding myself able to understand and predict more and more what you will be telling us in next report.

The clarity of your explanations and the no-nonsense approach you take resonated really well with my engineering background. I loved how you talked numbers without hiding behind the lingo or the empty words. The track of record of your portfolios speaks a million words. I dare any mutual fund to beat that.

— ALESSANDRO CATORCINI

To see dozens of other testimonials about *Terry's Tips* and the *Mighty Mesa Strategy*, go to **www.TerrysTips.com/Testimonials**.

The
MIGHTY
MESA

*A Tested Options Strategy
Designed to Never* Lose Money
(and Just Might Make 36%)*

Dr. Terry F. Allen

*Based on a 10-Year back test of S&P 500 volatility which showed no losses over any consecutive 12-month period (including the 9/11/01 and 10-11/08 market melt-downs).

Fuller Mountain Press
256 Fuller Mountain Road
Ferrisburgh, VT 05456

Printed in the United States

Library of Congress Control Number: 2006937199

ISBN – 978-0-9776372-5-6

Although the author has extensively researched appropriate sources to ensure the accuracy and completeness of the information contained in this publication, the author and the publisher assume no responsibility for errors, inaccuracies, omissions, or any inconsistency herein.

This publication is designed to provide accurate and authoritative information in regard to the subject matter covered. It is sold with the understanding that neither the author nor the publisher is engaged in rendering legal, tax, accounting, investment, or other professional services. No such advice is intended or implied. Neither the author nor the publisher is a registered investment advisor.

Options involve risk and are not suitable for all investors. Option trading involves substantial risk. You can lose money trading options. All investors who deal with options should read and understand "Characteristics and Risks of Standardized Options." A free copy of this publication can be obtained from The Options Clearing Corporation, One North Wacker Drive, Suite 500, Chicago IL 60606. 312-322-6200.

All securities named in this publication have been included purely for purposes of illustration. No recommendations to buy, sell, or hold such securities, or any securities, is intended. Readers should use their own judgment. If advice or other expert assistance is required, the services of a competent professional should be sought.

*This book is dedicated to my wife, Debbie,
the love of my life and my best friend,
. . . . and to Andrew, Floery, Heather,
Heidi, Jared, Seth and Shannon who
somehow manage to make each day
a daring adventure.*

Contents

Rule No.1: Never lose money.
Rule No.2: Never forget rule No.1.

— WARREN BUFFETT

Introduction

For many years, I have been dismayed at the dismal returns most people made with their conventional investments. I knew from my 30 years of total immersion in the world of stock options that better returns were possible.

In September 2008 I started writing this little book to explain the strategy that I had developed and perfected over those years of trading and study. I call it the *Mighty Mesa* because of the shape of the risk profile graph that the strategy creates at the beginning of each expiration month. (See the back cover for a picture of a risk profile graph.)

The first thing I did was to back test the strategy for the past 10 years, using the monthly fluctuations in the S&P 500 (SPY) as the data source. The results were dramatic — there was not a single twelve-month period when the strategy showed a loss, and the average annual gain was over 36% (after all commissions).

When people refer to "the" market, they usually mean the S&P 500. It is one of the most stable of all indexes. Over the ten-year back test, its worst month was a drop of 16.7% when the terrorist attack on 9/11 occurred. Only six times out of 120 expiration months did SPY fluctuate by a double-digit percentage.

And then came October 2008. SPY fell by over 23%. It was called the "most volatile month in the 80-year history of the S&P 500" by the New York Times. While I'm getting a little ahead of my story, you should know that the *Mighty Mesa Strategy* does best when the market is absolutely flat. Volatility is the Darth Vader of the strategy.

I knew that the *Mighty Mesa Strategy* would face the ultimate test in October 2008. If the strategy could survive this month, it could probably survive anything. At the very least, maybe it wouldn't be tested again to that extent for another 80 years.

Fortunately, I had set up an actual portfolio to test the *Mighty Mesa* in July 2008 for the subscribers of my *Terry's Tips* option newsletter

You begin by always expecting
good things to happen.

— TOM HOPKINS

to follow. I told subscribers of every trade made in this account as it was made so they could mirror it in their own accounts if they wished (and hundreds of them did).

The portfolio suffered a big loss in October 2008 as was to be expected with such extreme volatility. However, the portfolio gained enough money in both the September and November expiration months to more than cover the October loss. For the three-month period that included the extreme October volatility (and the big down market in November as well), the portfolio gained at better than the 36% annualized rate which the strategy achieved over the 10-year back test.

During this period, investors in mutual funds and individual stocks saw their portfolios fall by 40% or more. Meanwhile, followers of the *Mighty Mesa* were counting their winnings. For *Terry's Tips'* subscribers, it was a time for great celebration all around.

The actual stock portfolio employing this *Mighty Mesa Strategy* is called *Mighty Stalagmite*. A *stalagmite* is an upward-growing massive calcite mound. This seems to be the perfect description for how this portfolio should unfold. No matter how much rain falls, no matter how bad the market gets, the original base should remain intact. In fact, falling water is crucial to the growth of a stalagmite.

In the past six years of publishing *Terry's Tips*, I have made several modifications of the basic strategy that I advocated. Each iteration of the strategy caused it to become more conservative.

At the beginning, the goal was to achieve annual returns of 100%. Many times we were successful. Every trade I made was in an actual account for all my subscribers to see — no trades were swept under the rug. I like to think that total transparency is an important difference between my newsletter service and many others out there.

While we often made extraordinary returns, there were times when the market fell precipitously (or whipsawed wildly) and we forfeited most (or all) that we had gained for the past several months. Clearly, a more dependable strategy was in order, one which did not have the roller-coaster rides of the past six years.

You cannot open a book
without learning something.

— CONFUCIUS

How far we have come — from seeking 100% annual gains to constructing a portfolio designed to never lose money (and just make 36%). While there may be some minor tweaks yet to be made to the *Mighty Mesa Strategy*, I firmly believe that the main ingredients are pretty much set in stone.

I want to acknowledge, and thank, Kevin Deegan, an insightful and rare (because he understands options) stockbroker from Las Vegas for his important contribution to the current configuration of the *Mighty Mesa Strategy*. (He is also pretty smart — he warned his clients in advance both of the 1987 and 2008 market meltdowns.)

I have tried to make this an easy book to read. First, I describe the *Mighty Mesa Strategy* as simply as possible, without using technical option terminology. For those of you who would like more of the technical mumbo-jumbo, Appendix A contains a short discussion of the "Greeks" as they are known in the trade.

Second, I have spiced up the sometimes weighty discussion of stock options with some of my favorite quotations on business and life.

All I ask of you is to learn how to construct a simple risk profile graph (software makes this task easy) and to understand two kinds of option spreads, a calendar spread, and what I call a custom butterfly spread.

Already, I know that the word "spread" may be Greek to most people. Most of us think of a spread as the expanse of someone's belly or the land around the farmhouse, or something that goes on toast. An options spread is a little different, and I will do my best to follow Einstein's advice, and keep it as simple as it is, but not simpler.

While it would be nice if the *Mighty Mesa Strategy* were more simple than it is, I am secretly delighted that it is a bit complex, and essentially incomprehensible to most people. Otherwise, everyone would be using it.

Will Rogers said that everyone is ignorant only about different subjects. When I decided to make stock options my life work, I think I picked a subject where just about everyone was a little ignorant, and after 30 years of study, I might be a little less ignorant than most of them.

If you want to be successful,
find someone who has achieved the results
you want and copy what they do
and you'll achieve the same results.

— TONY ROBBINS

This book is a modified and updated version of another book I wrote in 2007 with a revised edition in 2008 — *Making 36%: Duffer's Guide to Breaking Par in the Market Every Year in Good Years and Bad*. The *Mighty Mesa* includes an exotic spread that is designed to eliminate the losses that occurred when the market made exceptionally large fluctuations in a single expiration month in the strategy described in *Making 36%*.

I decided to self-publish this book rather than send if off to a traditional publisher. I have been disappointed by the marketing efforts made by major houses (such as John Wiley) who have published other books I have written. I felt that this book was too important for me to hand over to someone else.

Publishing a book myself has some downsides, however. I have been totally discounted by the financial press because I have the audacity to claim possible returns that are far above what "everyone" knows is possible. I sent review copies of *Making 36%* to every major financial publication (and as many minor ones as I could find) and *not one single publication would write a review.* Apparently, no one wants to take the risk that I would ultimately turn out to be a charlatan, and they would be discredited somewhere down the line.

The biggest difficulty I have had in selling this book is my credibility. I have simply promised too much. It doesn't seem to matter much that I have actually achieved these gains, and much more, for several years. Both for myself and my *Terry's Tips* subscribers.

Now that you have found this book, I feel a tremendous responsibility to not disappoint you. If you have any questions about options, I will try to answer them; email me at **Terry@TerrysTips.com**. (For information about becoming a subscriber, call 800-803-4595.) I am not a licensed investment advisor, so I can't offer you advice on your personal investments, but I can answer most questions concerning options. I hope you enjoy reading this book as much as I enjoyed writing it. I look forward to prospering with you.

Part I

The
STOCK MARKET
WORLD

It is difficult to make predictions,
especially when they involve the future.

— NAMELESS SAGE

CHAPTER 1

Whither Goeth the Market?

Thomas Friedman, in *The World is Flat*,[1] explained how the entire world has become flat, and why it will continue to become flatter in the future. He could have said the same thing about stock markets.

Some of the smartest people in the world see flat markets ahead. Warren Buffet, America's most successful investor, writing in 2004, said that he expects at least 10 years of flat markets.[2]

In 2006, Robert Arnott said "15 years from now, stock prices won't be materially higher than they are today."[3]

Value Line predicts three to five years of flat markets.[4] One of the most accurate of all long-term market-timing models is the one based on projections from analysts at *Value Line* for price changes over the next three to five years for the 1,700+ stocks they monitor. While their short-term forecasts have not been particularly accurate, their longer-term predictions have been remarkably on the money for over 30 years.

The *Value Line* three to five year projections are extremely valuable for many reasons:

1) Their analysts are independent and immune from the pressures that can be found in research departments associated with investment banks and brokerage firms.
2) Few other firms besides *Value Line* even bother to focus on what will happen in three to five years, concentrating instead on just the next 12 months.

1. Thomas L Friedman, *The World is Flat: A Brief History of the Twenty-First Century* (New York: Farrar, Straus and Giroux, 2005)
2. Quoted by Rich Karlgaard, *Forbes*, October 4, 2004.
3. Robert D. Arnott, chairman of Research Affiliates (*New York Times*, October 1, 2006 article by Paul J. Lim).
4. Mark Hulbert, *New York Times*, July 18, 2004.

Those who have knowledge, don't predict.
Those who predict, don't have knowledge.

— Lao Tzu,
6th Century BC Chinese Poet

3) The large number of stocks they cover means that random errors in individual stocks become insignificant. (The indicator is the median projection of almost 2000 separate forecasts). Analyst errors on individual stocks tend to cancel each other out.

When *Value Line* predicts lower or flat markets in three to five years, we all should take notice.

Some observers see a slightly better scenario than a flat market. John Bogle, founder of the Vanguard and one of the most respected professionals in the financial world, makes a sound argument that future stock market returns will average about 7% rather than the 10%+ plus returns of the last 50 years or so. His argument is based on the fact that much of the past gains came about because average P/E ratios rose over that time period, and we cannot assume that they will continue to rise. In fact, he argues that these ratios are more likely to fall than they are to go up even further.[5]

John Bogle found support for this forecast from other substantial sources — "When Henry McVey, market strategist for Morgan Stanley, polled the chief financial officers of the 100 largest corporations in the United States, they expected a future return on stocks of only 6.6 percent".

Bogle also quotes Gary P. Brison, former president of UBS Investment Management — "Today's investment market fundamentals and financial variables clearly suggest that future real returns are unlikely to be greater than 4.5 or 5.0 percent."

(Note: I wrote the above in September 2008. Over the subsequent two months, markets lost over 40% of their value, and the S&P 500 hit an 11-year low. It is likely to be a long time before the market even catches up to where it was just a short time ago.)

So let's face it. Markets are likely to be flat, or at best, moderately higher for the next several years. How will you cope with this new reality? Where will you put your money? One thing is certain — what has worked in the past will surely not work in the future. You can't

5. Bogle, John C., *The Little Book of Common Sense Investing* (John Wiley & Sons, 2007).

The only thing we know about the future is that it will be different.

— Peter Drucker

just buy the market and hope prices will go up. Anyone who owned stocks or mutual funds in the fall of 2008 knows this very well, as they saw their net worth fall by 40% from what it was just one year earlier.

In this little book, I will explain an options strategy where maximum gains come in flat markets. In fact, I will prove mathematically that if the market stays absolutely flat, the strategy will make over 100% a year. Then I will show how it can dependably make 36% every year even when the market fluctuates up and down as we all know it is likely to do.

Just as important, based on the 10-year back test of SPY volatility (and reinforced by the experience in late 2008), the *Mighty Mesa* strategy did not show a single loss for any consecutive 12-month period. Some readers probably wish they had read this book earlier than they did.

You don't own stocks. Stocks own you.

— Tony Balis,
Founder, www.HUMANITY.ORG

CHAPTER 2

Buying Stocks and Mutual Funds

When most people think about investing, I suspect their first thoughts usually focus on individual stocks or mutual funds. Of course, there are a plethora of other investment opportunities, such as bonds, real estate, or a business of your own, but these are minor alternatives compared to the gigantic world of stocks and mutual funds.

I also suspect that most people would not even think of stock options as a viable investment alternative, and since you have picked up this book, that means that you are one giant step ahead of most everyone else. Congratulations!

It is the basic premise of this book that investing in individual stocks or mutual funds is a pretty dumb thing to do (with one possible exception, to be noted shortly).

People who buy stocks or mutual funds must believe that they can pick winners. While they know they would not have a chance against a professional tennis player, they somehow believe that they can pick stocks at least as well as professional investment managers.

In this book, I acknowledge that I am asking you to take a great leap of faith. I have taken the position that the *Mighty Mesa Strategy* has *less* risk than conventional stock and mutual fund investments, and at the same time, can be expected to generate profits which are two or three times greater than those "normal" investments. I understand that such a statement is contrary to the basic principle of investing that risk and reward are correlated. But that is what I believe, and I have documented results to support my belief.

Non-Professional Investment Decisions

How smart are non-professional individuals when it comes to making investment decisions? At least they are consistent. When it comes to the best time to get in or get out, ordinary investors have collectively been dead wrong every time.

Don't gamble! Take all your savings
and buy some good stock and hold it till it goes up,
then sell it. If it don't go up, don't buy it.

— WILL ROGERS

One of the best indicators as to which way the market is headed is to look at what individual investors are doing, and do just the opposite. The supporting facts are overwhelming.

When stocks were cheap in 1990, individuals invested only $18 billion in equity funds. In 1999 and 2000 when they were extremely over-valued, they poured $420 billion into equity funds only to lose about 40% over the next couple of years. What's more, they also overwhelmingly chose the highest-risk growth funds to the virtual exclusion of more conservative value-oriented funds. "While only 20 percent of their money went into risky aggressive growth funds in 1990, they poured a full 95 percent into such funds during 1999 and 2000. After the fall, when it was too late, investor purchases dried up to as little as $50 billion in 2002, when the market hit bottom."[1]

Driven by the mirror emotions of fear or greed, individuals look at the most recent past, and decide whether to invest or not to invest based on that recent past. They do the same thing with mutual funds. When a particular fund has posted exceptional returns, investors pile into that fund. The record shows that over half of last year's top-performing mutual funds actually do worse than the average in the years following their unusual good results.

Something to Think About

Have you ever thought about who is on the other side of any trade you make in the market?

Professional investors — financial institutions, mutual funds, investment banks, hedge funds, etc. — collectively account for about 90% of stock market volume.[2] These are the real professionals. They have more resources, more access to inside information, more money than you, and their decisions are made by the brightest, best-paid, full-time and highly-educated people that money can buy.

Every time you make a trade in the market, the chances are about nine out of ten that the other side of the transaction is taken by one

1. Bogle, John C., *The Little Book of Common Sense Investing* (John Wiley & Sons, 2007).
2. Charles D. Ellis, *Winning the Loser's Game,* (New York: McGraw-Hill, 2002).

People exaggerate their own skills.
They are overoptimistic about their
prospects and overconfident about
their guesses, including which
(investment) managers to pick.

— Professor Richard Thaler, University of Chicago

of these smart professionals who has all the resources that you are lacking.

So if you are buying, they are selling. If you are selling, they are buying. Just think about that next time you place an order to buy or sell some stock.

When you buy a stock, it is usually because you have just read an article or two about the company, or received a tip from a friend or broker. When a professional buys a stock, it is usually after extra-ordinary research, including talking with top management of the company (and top management of competitors), talking to customers of these companies, monitoring of supply chain and industry developments, attending trade association meetings, tracing inventory trends, consulting economists, industry specialists, securities analysts and other experts.

Just because the professionals do 20 times as much research as you do before making an investment decision doesn't mean they will always be right and you will be wrong. But who do you think has the better odds of being right?

You can easily select the absolute best car to buy, but if you pay too much, it really is not a good deal. The same is true for stocks, and the person who is selling you the stock knows a whole lot more about it than you do.

Buying Individual Stocks

Once you have shelled out your cash to bet on a single company, if any of the following takes place, your stock will most likely go down in value:

- An analyst down-grades the stock.
- The company fails to meet expected quarterly earnings.
- The company achieves expected earnings but fails to meet the "whisper" numbers.
- The company meets the "whisper" earnings number but falls short of sales expectations.

You can never predict when that unknown
torpedo will come out of the dark
and smash the price of a stock.

— RALPH SEGER

- The company meets the "whisper" numbers but issues a gloomy outlook for the future.
- The company gets hit with a lawsuit.
- The company is accused of corporate shenanigans:
- Cooking the books
- Back-dating management stock options grants
- Selling unsafe products (and knowing about them)
- Patent infringement
- Etc.
- The company loses a big contract to a competitor.
- A company in the same industry or sector does any of the above, or has a bad quarter, or issues a gloomy outlook, or whatever
- The market as a whole falls, taking down most stocks with it.

If you own stock in an individual company, any of the above things (and many more) can happen to your stock at any time. And probably ruin your day. When you own an individual stock, you are sitting on a financial time bomb.

On the other hand, if you own a broad-based Exchange Traded Fund (ETF) like the S&P 500 SPDRS (SPY) or the Russell 2000 (small cap — IWM), you only have to worry about a general market decline. If this happens, you will be moaning along with everyone else.

No one likes a falling stock portfolio. But it is a whole lot less painful when everyone else is in the same boat.

The bottom line is that owning an individual stock is a risky bet that probably has a slightly better than 50-50 chance of going up. You might get lucky and make some money, but most of the time you will not beat the market averages.

If you insist on buying individual stocks regardless of the miserable odds of being successful, there is an options strategy that works better than the outright purchase of the stock. I call it the *Shoot Strategy* (as in shoot for the stars). If the stock goes up, the strategy will result in far greater percentage gains than if you had bought the

*Individuals should not be buying
individual stocks. They should assume
that the information and advice they
receive regarding individual stocks are
stale and, to a large degree, already
incorporated in the stock price.*

— DAN REINGOLD,
CONFESSIONS OF A WALL STREET ANALYST

stock instead. And if the stock stays flat, you will make a small profit — something you wouldn't make if you just owned the stock.

At *Terry's Tips*, in November 2007 we started five actual accounts to demonstrate this strategy, each account trading options on a different underlying stock. Nine months later, the composite option portfolios had gained over 20% after commissions while the general market (S&P 500) had fallen by over 10%.

About a year after these accounts were set up, the market crashed, and these portfolios were in the red, but had lost less than half as much as the market in general (the S&P 500). (These portfolios are updated each week at *Terry's Tips*, and subscribers can see every trade ever made in them). The *Shoot Strategy* is explained in Appendix F.

Buying Mutual Funds

Millions of Americans understand the unlikely odds that they can pick individual stocks better than the professionals. So they hire the professionals to do it for them by purchasing (usually actively-managed) mutual funds. Since the fund invests in a large number of companies, these folks think they are making a prudent investment by spreading their risk and becoming diversified. They usually feel even better because they have probably picked a mutual fund that had a great record over the past year or five years.

I have one question to ask anyone who buys a mutual fund — why would you put your hard-earned money into an investment that has a 75% chance of losing?

Charles Ellis in *Winning the Loser's Game* reports that — "The historical record is that on a cumulative basis, over three-quarters of professionally managed funds *under*performed the S&P 500 Stock Average . . . over the past 50 years, mutual funds have lost 180 basis points — compounded annually — compared to the S&P 500."

He continues, "Even more disconcerting . . . the average mutual fund investor gets a return that is significantly below the return of the average mutual fund. From 1984 to 1995 the investors' shortfall was a stunning 6% annually, almost one-half of the 12.3% 'earned' by

By day we write about "Six Funds to Buy NOW!" . . . By night, we invest in sensible index funds. Unfortunately, pro-index fund stories don't sell magazines.

— Anonymous Fortune Magazine Writer

the average equity mutual fund, . . . The reason: frequent trading or turnover. Instead of staying the course with their investments, many investors tried to time the market, holding a fund for less than three years before selling and buying something else."[3]

How would you make out if you only bought the highest-ranking mutual funds? *Morningstar* is the most respected source — each year they rank all the mutual funds from one-star (the worst) to five-stars (the best). If you purchased only five-star rated funds, you would find that in the following year, over 50% of those funds would underperform the S&P 500. Regression to the mean is a much more powerful likelihood than a continuation of the exceptional returns for the prior year.[3]

John Bogle is considered to be the father of the index fund industry. He is known as the man who left over $20 billion on the table when he set up the Vanguard Group as a "mutual" rather than taking it public or owning it outright himself (which he could have done). In 2007, he published *The Little Book of Common Sense Investing*.[4]

The essential message of the book was summed up in a single sentence — "During the past 25 years, while the stock market index fund was providing an annual return of 12.3 percent and the average equity *fund* was earning an annual return of 10.0 percent, the average fund *investor* was earning only 7.3 percent a year."

The index fund outperformed the average mutual fund because of management fees, turnover costs including commissions (the average holding period for a mutual fund is about a year while the index fund essentially never sells), and capital gains taxes incurred when stocks were sold. The average fund investor lagged the average mutual fund because of adverse timing and fund selection decisions by individuals.

I encourage you to read John Bogle's little book. I can't believe that any rational person could read this book and ever buy a mutual fund again (unless it is a broad market index fund with the lowest management fee). It is as simple as that.

3. Ibid
4. Op. Cit., Bogle

In my opinion, investing in a diversified portfolio of mutual funds ranks among the worst possible investments.

— ROBERT KIYOSAKE,
CO-AUTHOR *RICH DAD, POOR DAD*

Bogle quotes other people who have commented on the performance of mutual funds —

"The truth is, for the most part, fund managers have offered extremely poor value for money. Their records of outperformance are almost always followed by stretches of underperformance." The *Economist* of London

"The investment business is a giant scam. Most people think they can find managers who can outperform, but most people are wrong." — Jack R.Meyer, former president of Harvard Management Company

"A minuscule 4 percent of funds produce market-beating after-tax results with a scant 0.6 percent (annual) margin of gain. The 96 percent of funds that fail to meet or beat the Vanguard 500 Index fund lose by a wealth-destroying margin of 4.8 percent per annum." — David Swensen, chief investment offices of the Yale University Endowment Fund

If mutual fund managers really can't outperform the market, why do we pay them so much? Year after year, millions of investors pay mutual fund managers billions of dollars to underperform the market. It's one of the investment world's strangest mysteries. Does it make sense to you?

Jack Bogle and Charley Ellis are not alone in recommending index funds —

- Warren Buffet said in his *Berkshire Hathaway Annual Report* in 1996, "Most investors...will find that the best way to own common stocks is through an index fund that charges minimal fees."
- "Most individual investors would be better off in an index mutual fund." — Peter Lynch
- "Most of my investments are in equity index funds." — William F. Sharpe, Nobel Laureate in Economics, 1990
- Even a famous stock broker agrees; "Most of the mutual fund investments I have are index funds, approximately 75%." — Charles R. Schwab

Day trader's prayer:
"Please, God, let me break even today.
I could really use the money."

— ROBERT QUILLEN

A $10,000 investment in 1982 in an index fund matching the S&P 500 grew to $109,000 by the end of 2002, while an identical investment in the average managed stock fund would have grown to $63,600. The reason: While the S&P 500 returned 12.7% a year, costs reduced the average stock fund's annual return to 9.7%.[5]

What further proof do you need that non-index mutual funds are one of the worst places to put your money? Yet I'll bet that most readers of this book own mutual funds. As Charley Ellis points out, "Las Vegas is busy every day, so we know that not everyone is rational."

When I first read Bogle's book (in the summer of 2008), I was tempted to shift a large portion of my investments to a Vanguard index fund, and I almost did. I only changed my mind after I studied the *Mighty Mesa Strategy* that is designed to never* lose money and decided that it would be a safer choice. My decision was vindicated a few months later when the broad-market index funds lost 40% of their value from the prior year and my *Mighty Mesa* portfolio investments made substantial gains.

As I write this, I do not own a single share of stock, or any bonds or mutual funds. The only CD I own plays music. I have cast my entire retirement lot with the *Mighty Mesa Strategy*. (I do own an interest in a venture capital partnership and some commercial real estate, but I am trying to sell both of them so that I can add more money to the *Mighty Mesa* portfolios.)

I subscribe to the motion first set out by Mark Twain and later adopted by Andrew Carnegie to put all your eggs in one basket, and then watch the basket carefully.

5. Weekend Interview with Jack Bogle, *Wall Street Journal,* September 2–3, 2006.

*Contrary to their oft articulated goal of
outperforming the market averages, investment
managers are not beating the market;
the market is beating them.*

— Charles D. Ellis

CHAPTER 3

Pity the "Experts" Who Just Don't Know

Dr. Simon Ramo, writing in *Extraordinary Tennis for the Ordinary Tennis Player,*[1] said that in professional tennis, about 80% of points resulted from winning shots, while in amateur tennis, about 80% of points were the result of one player making a mistake. Professional tennis is a winner's game, while amateur tennis is a loser's game.

My graduate school classmate, Charley Ellis, in his delightful and valuable investment guide, *Winning the Loser's Game,* extended Ramo's observation to the investment world: "Likewise, the 'money game' we call investment management has evolved in recent decades from a winner's game to a loser's game . . . In just 40 years the market activities of the investing institutions shifted from only 10% of total public transactions to an overwhelming 90% . . . No longer was the active investment manager competing with cautious custodians or amateurs who were out of touch with the market: Now he or she was competing with other experts in a loser's game where the secret to winning is to lose less than the others lose."[2]

The end result is that the professionals increasingly behave more like lemmings than they do original-thinking entrepreneurs.

In this little book, I will show you a simple system using options that will allow you to win the loser's game by increasing your odds of investment success. When you buy a stock, your odds of winning are a little better than 50% (since most stocks eventually go up).

Once you understand how the *Mighty Mesa* works you considerably increase your odds of winning the loser's game. Not only will you make greater gains when the stock goes up, but you will also prosper if the stock stays absolutely flat, and you can also gain if the stock falls (as long as it doesn't fall too much).

1. Simon Ramo, *Extraordinary Tennis for the Ordinary Tennis Player,* (New York: Crown Publishers, 1977).
2. Charles D. Ellis, *Winning the Loser's Game,* (New York: McGraw-Hill, 2002).

To my broker — even if he has,
from time to time, made me just that.

— ANDREW TOBIAS,
THE ONLY INVESTMENT GUIDE YOU WILL EVER NEED

Doctors bury their mistakes.
Brokers just take a second commission.

— UNKNOWN

Pity Your Broker

The poor sucker just doesn't know. He is trying his best to make you happy and keep his job, but it is all a crap shoot. He knows all too well that he just doesn't know, and the monkeys throwing the darts will do just as well as he does. And yet he is required to pretend that he does know.

Sounds like an ulcer-producing job to me.

Remember that your broker does not make money *for* you — he makes it *from* you.

Your broker loves it when you bring a stock to him. He can tell you that the stock is not on his firm's "Buy" list, but he secretly hopes you will buy it anyway so he makes a commission and it was your idea. You have let him (and his analysts) off the hook. He loves you. Good work!

Your broker will most certainly never tell you about trading options. Some reasons:

- He doesn't know anything about option trading (for years, I have been dismayed by the utter lack of understanding that most brokers have about options — no matter how educated or experienced they might be).
- Commission rates at full-service brokers are too high for you to make money trading options, especially the kind of spreads I recommend (each spread involves two commissions).
- Everyone "knows" that options are extremely risky. Since most options expire worthless, option traders must be losing their shirts. If he recommends options to you, and you lose money, you may sue him. He wants to keep his job.

Your broker is probably a really nice guy. He may even be your favorite golfing buddy. Don't embarrass him by showing him this book. He will tell you that it is a bunch of crap. If enough people start trading the *Mighty Mess Strategy* he will be out of a job. This book is a threat to his very existence.

*Wall Street, with its army of brokers,
analysts, and advisers funneling trillions
of dollars into mutual funds,
hedge funds, and private equity funds,
is an elaborate fraud.*

— MICHAEL LEWIS

The Analysts

If brokers really don't know which are the best stocks to buy, how about the analysts? After all, they don't have to spend most of their time schmoozing with investors like you. It's their job to do thorough investigations of companies, the industry, and competitors, and make recommendations that they can pass on to the brokers who then pass them on to you.

Unfortunately, the analysts are ultimately not much good for you either. In similar fashion to brokers, their primary motivation is job security. The way to do that is to come up with "findings" that are pretty much the same as the other analysts. That way, if they are wrong, they can point to all the other supposedly brilliant analysts who came up with the same conclusion. Even when they're all wrong, they will probably keep their jobs

The sad truth is that if 20 out of 22 analysts rate XYZ a "buy" or a "strong buy," that is probably an excellent reason to *sell* the stock.

Most of those analysts' clients have already bought the stock. They did it when the analyst first made his or her recommendation. There may not be many people left to buy the stock.

On the other hand, if an analyst downgrades the stock, all hell breaks loose. If 20 out of 22 analysts have already put out a "buy" recommendation, the odds are ten to one that any change in their assessment will be on the downside. And downgrades kill a stock.

A couple of years ago, I searched for a stock that was likely to be a real dog. I wanted to find a company that had a very good chance of falling, or at least was very unlikely to go up. My goal was to set up an options strategy that would make 100% a year if the stock stayed flat (or fell by any amount). It is a relatively easy thing to do, actually, if the stock behaves as you expect, but that is another story.

I eventually found a stock that almost every analyst just hated. In one magazine article, five analysts were asked to select their single best short sale candidate. Two of them selected this same company — Dillard Department Stores (DDS). One analyst explained that "Dil-

*Estimates of security analysts aren't much
better than those that would be obtained
by simple extrapolation of past trends.*

— BURTON MALKIEL
IN *A RANDOM WALK DOWN WALL STREET*

lard can't compete with K-Mart or Wal-Mart on price, or get the margins of more upscale stores."

While most analysts rank companies as *strong buy*, *buy*, or *hold* (which is generally a euphemism for *sell*), an amazing 70% of analysts rated DDS as *sell* or *strong sell*. I had never seen such a universal condemnation of a company like this. Surely, Dillard was the dog of all dogs, just what I was looking for. Even its stock symbol reminded me of a root canal.

Over the next eight months, while the market in general *fell* by 8%, DDS *went up* by 50%. A year later, it was 100% higher than when the analysts picked it as their favorite short sale candidate. My option portfolio using the stock also suffered until I bit the bullet and closed it down.

I learned my lesson. Next time I find a stock that is so universally hated by the experts, I am more likely to buy it than sell it. But as you know, I don't think that buying (or selling) stock in individual companies is a very good idea in any event. I far prefer an option strategy that makes money regardless of whether the underlying stock goes up or down — like the *Mighty Mesa Strategy*.

If you wish to know the road up the mountain,
ask the man who goes back and forth on it.

— ZENRIN

CHAPTER 4
A Special Case – The Author

My name is Terry Allen. I am an options addict. I am old enough to collect Social Security, and I continue to trade options every day. I have traded options ever since they were "invented" in 1973. When I am not trading options, I am thinking about them. I even dream about options.

Along the way, I got an MBA from the Harvard Business School. A few years later I earned a Doctorate in Business Administration at the University of Virginia. While at Virginia, I lived in the computer lab, trying out various option strategies.

At the time, the publicly-traded options industry was just starting and option prices were quite inefficient. I created a computer model to help me make trading decisions. It was easy to make huge profits. I doubled my money every six months for two years while I was still a doctoral student.

Then I headed for Chicago. I leased a seat on the Chicago Board Options Exchange (CBOE) and traded on the floor. Then a couple of math professors named Black and Scholes developed and published a computer model that told everyone what option prices should be. (They later earned a Nobel Prize for their work.)

Their model was very much like the one I had created. It killed my golden goose. To this day, the Black-Scholes model (or one similar to it) is used by nearly all professional option traders. Option prices are now quite efficient. It is a much greater challenge to make extraordinary profits. But it is still possible.

In many years, I doubled my money trading options, but the most important years were those when I lost money. Those were the times when I really learned something. In fact, I would be suspicious of any options "expert" who has never had a bad year. He probably hasn't been in the business long enough to appreciate the deeper risks of option trading.

There is only one success — to be able
to spend your life in your own way.

— CHRISTOPHER MORLEY

My early success spoiled me. I believed that if I didn't make at least 100% every year, I was failing. It was not until recently that I altered my strategy so that I could pursue a more reasonable annual profit goal and have an extremely high likelihood of achieving it.

Trading options has been good to me. In the late 1990s, I set a goal of giving away an average of $1000 every day for the rest of my life to worthy Vermont charities. I built a swimming pool for the Burlington Boys & Girls Club. I have provided several hundred thousands of dollars in college scholarships for low-income Vermonters and single parents. So far, I have given away over $2,000,000 to more than 50 Vermont charities.

My wife and I built a "new" 200-year-old house using materials from several houses built before 1810, and "retired" to a remote 220-acre farm in Vermont. Debbie manages some extensive award-winning perennial gardens and has written a successful book on maintaining such gardens (when we built the house, I gave her an unlimited budget for gardens, and she managed to exceed it).

Living so far away from the rumors and noise of Wall Street insulates me from trying to form an opinion as to which way the market is headed. Fortunately, a basic premise of my options strategy is that I have no idea which way the market will move in the short run. (In the past, the biggest mistakes I made came when I thought I knew which way the market was headed.)

I rarely watch television (unless there is a ball of some sort being tossed about). When the Internet becomes too much of a distraction, I retreat even further to a writing cabin deep in the woods where a wood stove keeps me warm while I reflect on option strategies.

A couple of months each year, Debbie and I go on fairly long European hikes. In 2008, for example, we completed the Wainwright coast-to-coast walk across England, some 200 miles. I can work anywhere there is an Internet connection, and the time difference makes it possible for me to be tuned into the U.S. options market at the end of our hiking day.

Work like you don't need the money.
Love like you've never been hurt.
Dance like nobody's watching.

— Satchel Paige

In 2001, I created **www.TerrysTips.com**, an options investment newsletter, so that I could continue my charitable endeavors. I eventually ran several actual option portfolios with differing underlying stocks and risk profiles so my subscribers could see how different strategies work over time.

In 2005, the SEC brought suit against me for providing personalized advice to subscribers without being a licensed investment advisor. They also objected to a statement on my website that they believed was misleading. While not admitting nor denying guilt, I paid a $230,000 fine and have continued my investment newsletter, now being careful not to provide individual personalized advice or make potentially misleading statements.

So when I tell you that I have developed an options strategy that is designed to never lose money, and just might make over 36% every year, in good years and bad, I better be pretty sure that the statement is supported by strong evidence.* I know the SEC is looking over my shoulder.

My goal in this book is to teach you that strategy without your having to become an options nut like me to carry it off. I wish us both luck.

---

* Based on a 10-year back test of S&P 500 volatility which showed no consecutive 12-month losing periods, and an average annual gain of 36%. See Chapter 9 for details of the back test.

Part II

$

The
WORLD
of
OPTIONS

*Can anybody remember when the times
were not hard and money not scarce?*

— Ralph Waldo Emerson

CHAPTER 5

Stock Investing vs. Options Investing

I believe that stock option trading is the one arena where there is a level playing field for the individual investor and Wall Street. In fact, you can win this loser's game while the professionals cannot. The big guys can't even play. They need to place hundreds of millions of dollars for their clients. There is not enough liquidity in the option markets for their purposes.

There is, however, sufficient liquidity in the option markets to invest $100,000 or more. I have had $2 million invested many times in option strategies similar to the *Mighty Mesa Strategy* without incurring any problems with liquidity (if I picked the right underlyings).

There seems to be a niche in the options market for winning the loser's game — a niche too small for the big guys but plenty big enough for you and me.

The biggest differences between the world of stocks (or mutual funds) and the world of options can be explained in mathematical terms. Stocks change arithmetically and options change geometrically.

These generalizations can be made:

If your stock goes up by 2% in one month, your stock portfolio will go up by that same 2%. The same change will take place if the stock goes down. There will be a linear arithmetic relationship between stock prices and portfolio values.

If the underlying stock of your options portfolio goes up by 2%, your portfolio value might do just about anything. If you are using the *Mighty Mesa Strategy,* it will probably gain an average of 6%–10% for that month. It would make that same average gain if the stock stayed flat or fell by 2% as well. (The *Mighty Mesa Strategy* likes 2% monthly stock price changes regardless of which direction they go.)

For those of us who love options, the arithmetic world of stocks is boring. It is like watching grass grow. Just about anything is more exciting. Even watching mind-numbing sit-coms.

Take calculated risks.
That is quite different from being rash.

— George S. Patton

Let's compare the arithmetic changes in the stock portfolio with the expected geometric changes in a *Mighty Mesa* portfolio. These things are true:

1. If the underlying stock stays flat or goes up by 1%, 2%, 3%, or 4% during one expiration month, the portfolio value will increase by an average 4%–10% after commissions.
2. If the underlying stock stays flat or goes down by 1%, 2%, 3%, or 4% during one expiration month, the portfolio value will increase by an average 4%–10% after commissions.
3. If the underlying stock goes up or down by 5% during one expiration month, the portfolio value will most likely break even (on average).
4. If the underlying stock goes up or down by 6% or more during one expiration month, unless adjustments are made, the options portfolio will lose money, and that loss could be double or more the percentage loss in the underlying stock.
5. The greater the percentage change in the underlying, the greater the possible percentage loss of the options portfolio. If the underlying stock falls by 15% in one expiration month, unless adjustments are made, the options portfolio could lose 40%.

It is clear from these statements that an important part of successfully operating the *Mighty Mesa Strategy* is to have an effective adjustment strategy ready to implement in those months where the underlying stock is more than moderately volatile. Such adjustment tactics are critical. They alone will save the investor from the geometrical changes in portfolio value that might result if the stock moves significantly and no adjustments are made. (Chapter 11 discusses adjustments.)

If you get involved in the *Mighty Mesa* options strategy, some things are certain. First, you will feel lonely. Not one person in 100 will have any idea about what you are doing. You won't be able to trade war stories with your friends about the various horses (stocks) you placed

Since the dawn of capitalism,
there has been one golden rule:
"If you want to make money,
you have to take risks."

— Announcer, Opening line of the Nova Special,
The Trillion Dollar Bet

your money on last week. You won't care one whit about how well a single company does.

Second, you will pay at least ten times as much as your stock-picking friends pay for commissions. But you are safe here — your friends won't know.

Third, everyone will think that you are a gun-slinging wild speculator who doesn't have any idea about prudent investments. Some of them will probably assume that you are desperate, betting your last dollar on a long shot in hopes to catch up with them and their conservative stock, bond, mutual fund, and CD "investments."

On the other hand, there are some positives to the option alternative. When the market stays flat (even though it moves up and then back down as it usually does), your friends will not have made any money at all while you might easily have made more than they make in an entire year. This simple possibility should be reason enough to take a closer look at the *Mighty Mesa* alternative.

There will be times when the market tanks and your option portfolio actually makes money. Those are the most delicious times of all.

So, bottom-line, if you don't care about your friends thinking you are a loner, and an imprudent and desperate speculator, and all you care about is making extraordinary returns every year regardless of what the market does, you can jump on the options bandwagon with me.

All I ask is that you put a small amount aside, say $10,000, and give it a try for three months. At the end of that time, you will have a better idea of whether or not you are a believer or not. If even this seems too risky, you could become a *Terry's Tips* Insider and watch several actual *Mighty Mesa* portfolios unfold over time before you plunk down any of your precious cash.

Options are Less Risky Than Stock

Most people believe that option players are extreme risk takers. After all, they purchase an asset with a very short life, and hope it skyrockets in value. Option buyers might make 500% or more if they buy the

It is not easy to get rich in Las Vegas,
at Churchill Downs or at the local
Merrill Lynch office.

— PAUL A. SAMUELSON

right option, just as they would do if they picked the winning horse at the track.

The waiting period to see if you're a big winner is a little longer than a horse race, but not much. In a month or two, if the stock does not go the way you guessed, you lose your entire investment. Just tear up your ticket. You picked the wrong horse.

If the stock stays flat, most option buyers lose most or all of their bet as well. No wonder people think that options trading is risky. At least if you buy a stock, and it stays flat, you don't lose anything but the opportunity to have done better with another investment.

When you buy an option, it is a declining asset. It depreciates faster than a new car. It becomes worthless in a matter of months.

High-risk, high-reward — that is an investment fact embraced by most people. Conventional wisdom says that any system that offers the opportunity for extraordinary profits must necessarily involve an inordinately high degree of risk.

Nothing could be further from the truth when it comes to intelligent options trading.

I am reminded of the ancient story of the blind men examining an elephant — each man touched a single part of the animal, and came to an entirely different conclusion as to what it was.

Viewed as single transactions, the following two statements are undeniably true:

1) Buying stock options is extremely risky.

Options decline in value every day the stock stays flat. Most options expire absolutely worthless, and the person who bought them loses his or her entire investment.

2) Selling stock options is even more risky.

Selling stock options, when viewed as a single transaction, is even worse. Selling an option alone is called selling naked (because that's how you feel the whole time you have that position in your account).

When you bet on a sure thing — hedge!

— Robert Half

You have the theoretical possibility of unlimited loss. You can lose many times more money than you invested. At least at the horse race, you only lose the money you bet.

No wonder people believe that stock options investing is risky. There seems to be extreme risk all around. Just like the blind men examining the elephant, they are only looking at a single part of the picture.

Since most people have not taken the time to understand stock options, they too quickly conclude that the risk level is too high for them, and put their money into a "safe" place like mutual funds. Somehow if they are paying some "expert" to pick the stocks they own, they delude themselves into believing they are investing prudently.

To my way of thinking, such conventional wisdom is naïve and erroneous. Below is a graph of what profit or loss will accrue in five weeks at different stock price points with a typical $10,000 investment in the *Mighty Mesa* (solid line) compared to the purchase of 100 shares of stock when the stock price is $72 (dotted line).

This graph clearly shows that the only way for the stock investment to make money is for the stock to go up by a healthy amount. If the stock goes down, the investment loses $100 for every dollar it falls.

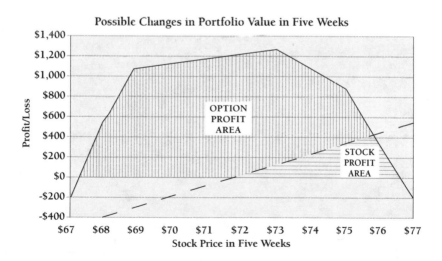

Possible Changes in Portfolio Value in Five Weeks

57

The early bird catches the worm,
but it is the second mouse who
gets the cheese.

— Unknown

However, if the stock goes down $3 in five weeks, the option portfolio still makes over 10% for the period while the stock investment loses 4%. If the stock goes up by $3, the stock investment gains 4% but the option portfolio gains more than double that amount. Which investment looks less risky to you?

If your money is in a mutual fund, even if it is an index fund, these are the facts:

1) If stocks go up, you will **make money** (but your profits will be reduced by the management fees, sales fees, and expenses you incur). For the past 50 years, the stock market has gained an average of about 10% a year. That is the most gain you should expect with your mutual fund investments. We have already seen that the average mutual fund investor has historically made only 6.3% a year. Furthermore, as we discussed earlier, most prognosticators expect lower annual returns in the future .
2) If stocks stay flat, you **lose money** (management fees and inflation reduce the value of your holdings).
3) If stocks go down in value, you **lose even more money**.

Contrast those facts with the case of a properly executed stock options strategy (such as the *Mighty Mesa*):

1) If the underlying stock goes up moderately, you **make money**, often at a rate of over 36% a year.
2) If the underlying stock stays flat, you **make money**, sometimes at a rate of over **100% a year**.
3) If the underlying stock goes down, you **may still make a profit**. Only if the stock fluctuates considerably in a very short time will you lose money. (Of course, your mutual fund would get clobbered if the stock fell significantly as well.)

Which of the above two investments is the most risky? It seems to me that the mutual fund investment is a whole lot riskier than the

If you don't know who you are,
the stock market is an expensive
place to find out.

— Adam Smith

stock options investment (not to mention that it yields a profit of only about one-sixth what the stock option portfolio might gain).

Why then does stock option investing get such a bad rap on the risk issue? People look at only a single part of the picture (buying or selling options) and ignore the total picture.

They conclude that if buying options is dangerous, and selling options is even more dangerous, then option trading must be doubly dangerous. **It does not occur to most people that a system of simultaneously buying and selling options might be even less risky than owning the stock**. This is the case, but most people never take the next step and learn the entire story.

The truth is that a properly-executed stock options strategy is considerably less risky than the purchase of stock or a mutual fund. However, it takes work. You will have to learn a little about how options work, and be an active part of the investment process. You can't plunk down your money like you do with a mutual fund and passively ignore your investment (although later in this book, I will show you how you can farm out the whole job to someone else).

The fact that stock options investing takes work discourages most people from even considering such an investment. That is fine with me. When I compare my returns each year with what the mutual funds are making, I feel like a real winner. I may work a little harder, but that's a small price to pay for the returns I make.

Transaction Costs for Stocks vs. Options

Transaction costs (commissions, bid-asked spread penalties, and management fees) are the bane of the investment world. This is particularly true for options because costs are much greater than they are for stock.

Study after study has shown that the more active an investor is, the more he buys and sells stocks, the worse off he becomes. Transaction costs essentially kill the active investor.

If stocks have averaged about 10% a year in gains over the long term and an investor pays out 2% in transaction costs, he has lost

October. This is one of the singularly
most dangerous months to speculate in stocks.
Others are November, December, January, February,
March, April, May, June, July, August and September.

— MARK TWAIN

20% of his gain. In the world of stock and mutual fund purchases, transaction costs are indeed significant concerns.

The situation is entirely different in the world of options (and at first sight, considerably worse, especially if the *Mighty Mesa Strategy* is followed). Option transaction costs are much higher for several reasons. The biggest challenge is the bid-asked spread penalty. The spread between the bid price and the asked price is usually much greater for options than it is for stocks.

The option trader usually must buy at the higher asked price and sell at the lower bid price. And in the *Mighty Mesa Strategy*, virtually every trade is a spread trade which involves two contracts instead of one, literally doubling the size of the bid-asked spread penalty and commission costs.

When a typical *Mighty Mesa* portfolio is established, the bid-asked spread penalty and commission cost is likely to be in the 3%–5% range. At the end of your first day of trading, your $10,000 investment appears to be worth only $9,600 on average, even if none of the option prices changed by a penny.

Pretty discouraging, isn't it? Most investors have been told that anything over 2% a year for transaction costs is just awful, and here we are looking at a 4% hit on Day One.

All commission costs are not equal. I'm not talking about the difference between full-service broker commissions (which may go into the hundreds of dollars) with a discount broker's rate, however. Comparing those kinds of commissions is at least an apples-to-apples comparison.

No, I'm talking about the significance of the commission you pay when you buy stock or a mutual fund and when you buy or sell an option. If you bought 100 shares of a $50 stock, you would shell out $5,000 plus about a $10 commission at your favorite discount broker. The only thing you know for certain about this purchase is that it ties up $5,010 that could be earning interest in a savings account.

A year later, unless the stock has increased in value, you still would not have covered the money you paid out for the commission. Even

*I like to buy (stock in) a business any
fool can run because eventually one will.*

— PETER LYNCH

though the commission works out to only 0.2% of the total investment, it is no wonder that commissions are a concern for the stock trader.

Contrast the stock purchase to the sale of a single option for $1.50 (a one-month at-the-money call or put option on SPY could be sold for almost double this amount, but let's take the lower number). On the $1.50 ($150) sale, *Terry's Tips* subscribers at *thinkorswim* would pay a commission of $1.50. This works out to 1% of the purchase price, or 5 times the percentage you would have paid to buy the stock.

However, the option seller has sold a depreciating asset that goes down in value every day. Over the course of the next month, the time premium of the option that was sold for $150 will depreciate by an average of $5 per day (so the person who sold that option will make an average $5 gain every day). In other words, in a single day after selling the option, if the stock price doesn't change, the commission cost will have been totally recovered three times over.

Of course, if a call was sold and the stock went up, the option that was sold for $150 might cost more to buy back the next day, but the option-seller presumably owns an off-setting longer-term call that will also increase in value. But the bottom line is the same — **every single day of the short option's life, the entire commission cost will be more than covered by the lowering value (decay) of the option**.

The buyer of stock might have to wait a year or more for the stock to go up and finally cover his commission cost while the option seller will cover his commission cost before lunch-time the following day.

In his mind, the option-seller should think of the commission cost as evidence that he has made a good investment that will pay for itself in less than a day. The more commissions you pay, the more decay you will be collecting.

This is just another example that the world of stock investing is far different from the world of option investing. While it may take a year to recover the commission you pay on a stock purchase, you would be disappointed if it took an entire day to recover that cost if you sold an option.

Save a little money each month,
and at the end of the year, you'll be
surprised at how little you have.

— ERNEST HASKINS

In spite of the extraordinary transaction costs of option trading, there are many option newsletters on the Internet which report their returns without recognizing commission costs. I can't understand how they stay in business.

It is best to think of transaction costs in an options portfolio as you would the interest costs of a commercial real estate investment. Interest might amount to 60% or more of your rental income, but if your net return was attractive, you wouldn't give the interest cost a second thought. It is only a necessary cost of owning that kind of investment.

Many people foolishly compare their commission costs in an option portfolio to the commission costs of trading stocks or mutual funds. That is a mistake. Anyone who focuses on transaction costs rather than the bottom line should not be trading options.

I believe the net gains from the *Mighty Mesa Strategy* should be far greater than virtually any mutual fund or real estate investment even after the extraordinarily high transaction costs are covered.

If you're not confused,
you're not paying attention.

— TOM PETERS

CHAPTER 6

Puts and Calls 101

H ere are the bare basic definitions of puts and calls. For a more
complete discussion of stock options, please check out Appendix A. If you are already familiar with the basics of puts and calls,
please feel free to skip over this chapter.

Basic Call Option Definition. Buying a *call option* gives you the
right (but not the obligation) to purchase 100 shares of a company's
stock at a certain price (called the strike price) from the date you buy
the call until the third Friday of a specific month (called the expiration date).

People buy *calls* because they hope the stock will go up, and they
will make a profit, either by selling the calls at a higher price, or by
exercising their option (i.e., buying the shares at the strike price when
the market price is higher).

Basic Put Option Definition. Buying a *put option* gives you the
right (but not the obligation) to sell 100 shares of a company's stock at
a certain price (called the strike price) from the date of purchase until
the third Friday of a specific month (called the expiration date).

People buy *puts* because they hope the stock will go down, and
they will make a profit, either by selling the puts at a higher price, or
by exercising their option (i.e., forcing the seller of the put to buy the
stock at the strike price at a time when the market price is lower).

LEAPS are long-term stock options. They have at least a year or
two of life. LEAPS is an acronym for Long-term Equity AnticiPationS.
All LEAPS expire in January.

Some Useful Details: Both put and call options are quoted in dollar terms (e.g., $3.50), but they actually cost 100 times the quoted
amount (e.g., $350), plus an average of $1.50 commission (charged
by my discount broker — commissions charged by other brokers may
be considerably higher).

All things are difficult before they are easy.

— THOMAS FULLER

Since most stock markets go up over time, and most people invest in stock because they hope prices will rise, there is more interest and activity in *call* options than there is in *put* options.

Real World Example of Call Options

Here are some call option prices for a hypothetical XYZ company on November 1, 2008 (price of stock: $45.00):

	Expiration Date			
Strike Price	Nov '08	Dec '08	Jan '10	Terminology of Option (price of call option)
40	$5.50	$7.00	$18.50	"in-the-money" (strike price is less than stock price)
45	$2.00	$4.00	$16.00	"at-the-money" (strike price is equal to stock price)
50	$0.50	$1.00	$14.00	"out-of-the-money" (strike price is greater than stock price)

The *premium* is the price a call option buyer pays for the right to be able to buy 100 shares of a stock without actually having to shell out the money the stock would cost. The greater the time period of the option, the greater the premium.

The premium (same as the price) of an in-the-money call is composed of the *intrinsic value* and the *time premium*. (I understand that this is confusing. For in-the-money options, the option price, or premium, has a component part that is called the time premium). The intrinsic value is the difference between the stock price and the strike price. Any additional value in the option price is called the time premium. In the above example, the Dec '08 40 call is trading at $7.00. The intrinsic value is $5 ($45 stock price less 40 strike price), and the time premium is $2.

For at-the-money and out-of-the-money calls, the entire option price is time premium. The greatest time premiums are found in at-the-money strike prices.

Greed is good.

— GORDON GEKKO

Decay is good.

— TERRY ALLEN

Call options are a way of leveraging your money. You are able to participate in any upward moves of a stock without having to put up all the money to buy the stock. However, if the stock does not go up in price, the option buyer may lose 100% of his/her investment. For this reason, buying options is considered by most people to be a risky investment.

As we will see soon, however, if you simultaneously buy and sell options, your resulting investment can be far less risky than owning stock or a mutual fund.

Decay Rate for a Typical Option

If the price of the stock remains the same, all options become less valuable over time. This makes total sense. If you own an option that has a year to go before it expires, you would be willing to pay more for it than you would for an option that lasted only a month.

The amount that the option falls in value is called its *decay*. There are two interesting aspects of decay. First, it tends to be quite low when there is a long time until the option expires. Second, decay increases dramatically as the option moves toward the date when it expires (the expiration date).

Below is a chart for a typical 12-month call option for a $70 stock. The strike price is $70 as well. If you were to buy this call option when it had 12 months until expiration, you would pay $7.80 ($780 per option). The stock would have to go up above $77.80 before you made a profit on the option if you held it until expiration.

Each month you waited to buy this option, you would pay less. The chart shows how much less the option would cost each month. If you bought the option when it only had one month to go before it expired, you would have to pay only $1.80, and the stock would only have to go up above $71.80 before you made a profit on the option.

Most option buyers prefer to pay $1.80 for an option that only has a month of remaining life rather than $7.80 for an option that has a year of life. In the *Mighty Mesa Strategy*, we do just the opposite.

*Education is what remains after one
has forgotten what one has learned in school.*

— ALBERT EINSTEIN

In the *Mighty Mesa Strategy,* at the same time we *buy* options with several months of remaining life until expiration, we *sell* someone else an option that only has a month to go until expiration. We are allowed to use our longer-term option as collateral for the short term sale.

The price we pay is the difference between the two options:

Buy one-year call option for $7.80
Sell one-month call option for $1.80
Cost of spread: $6.00 ($600)

After one month, if the price of the stock remains at $70, the price of the option we bought for $7.80 will have fallen in value by about $.40, and is then worth $7.40. However, the option we sold to someone else would be worthless since the stock price is not higher than $70 and there is no time remaining for the option.

The spread that we purchased for $6.00 is now worth $7.40. We made a gain of $1.40, or about 23% on our investment in a single month (less commissions). At that point, we would sell another one-month option for $1.80 and wait for another month to expire.

If the stock remained at $70 for an entire year, and we sold a one-month option 11 more times for $1.80 a pop, we would collect $19.80 ($1980) on our original investment of $6.00 ($600), or over 300%.

The difference in the lower decay rate of the long-term option we own and the higher decay rate of the short-term option we sell is the essence of the *Mighty Mesa*. Everything else is just details.

Of course, this is a simplified example. The stock will never stay exactly flat. Sometimes it will stay almost flat, however, and we would earn over 20% in a single month in the above example.

There are three aspects to the *Mighty Mesa Strategy:*

1) Place spreads similar to the above.
2) Buy "insurance" to protect against big stock moves. Like all insurance, it costs money and reduces our potential profits each month.
3) Make adjustments if there is a big price move (not always necessary).

To turn $100 into $110 is work.
To turn $100 million into $110 million is inevitable.

— EDGAR BRONFMAN, JR.

We don't mind giving up a bit of potential profit to dramatically increase the odds that a reasonable profit will come our way no matter what the stock does.

We only need 3% a month to achieve our goal of 36% a year. The above example shows that there is a potential gain of over 20% in a single month if the stock doesn't do much. As long as the insurance and adjustment costs are less than 17% of portfolio value each month, we will make our goal. In most cases, these costs are considerably less than 17% of the portfolio value.

You may wonder why a one-month option costs about three times as much as the average monthly cost of a one-year option. It is a matter of demand. Option buyers are risk-takers, much like lottery ticket buyers. They like to "wager" the smallest amount possible (regardless of the odds of winning), and the one-month option is their ticket of choice. Their demand pushes up the price of the shortest-term, least-expensive options. In many respects, when we employ the *Mighty Mesa Strategy,* we are like the house in Las Vegas, accepting wagers from the speculators, knowing that the odds are always in our favor.

Writing Covered Calls Doesn't Work

Many financial advisors and more than a dozen websites advocate writing (selling) covered calls as a sound investment strategy. Thousands of subscribers pay millions of dollars to get advice on profitable covered calls to write.

I believe they are wasting their money. Writing covered calls only limits the potential gain you might enjoy.

Let's take an example. You buy 100 shares of XYZ for $80 and write (sell) an at-the-money two-month call ($80 strike price) for $4.00. If the stock stays flat, you will earn 5% on your money for the period (plus collect a dividend if there is one). If you can do this six times a year (write a two-month call six times), you will earn 30% annually (less commissions); or so goes the promise.

"Wall Street," runs the sinister old gag,
"is a street with a river at one end
and a graveyard at the other."
This is striking, but incomplete.
It omits the kindergarten in the middle.

— FRED SCHWED

(Earlier in this chapter we showed that selling calls against a one-year option rather than stock results in a hypothetical 300% gain if the stock stays absolutely flat, or ten times the amount you could earn by writing calls against the stock.)

In this covered call-writing example, 30% is the maximum amount you can earn. No matter how high XYZ goes in price, you can never earn more than 30%. And **the bottom line truth is that you will NEVER earn that 30%**. The reason is that no stock price ever stays the same.

If the stock goes up by $5 in the first 60 days, you will either lose your stock (through exercise), or more likely, you will buy back the call you wrote, paying $5, and losing $1 on the call (but making $5 on the increase in the price of the stock). So for the first 60 days, you actually made a 5% net gain ($4 net gain on a $80 stock).

Presumably, you then sell another 60-day at-the-money call (now at the $85 strike) and collect perhaps $4.25. Then the stock falls back to $80. In this time period, you gain $4.25 from selling the call but you lose $5 in stock value for a net loss of $.75.

Your gains on the calls you wrote now total $3.25 for a 120-day period (you gained $4.00 in the first 60-day period and lost $.75 in the second). The stock is now just where it started (just what you hoped would earn you 30% for the year).

At this rate (four months of activity), your annual return will be $9.75, or 12.2% on the original $80 stock. Commissions on six sales of calls over the year will considerably reduce this return — to 10% or so. Not a bad return, but certainly not 30%. And it's an awful lot of work for a 10% return.

What is even better than writing covered calls? The *Mighty Mesa Strategy*, of course. This strategy can make over 36% a year in good years and bad. It involves buying longer-term options and selling short-term options against them at several different strike prices.

At the beginning of 2003, I put $10,000 in an account to demonstrate to *Terry's Tips* (my Internet newsletter) subscribers how a strategy of buying long-term options and selling short term options against

It's not whether you are right or wrong that's important, but how much money you make when you're right and how much you lose when you're wrong.

— George Soros

them might work. I called this the *10K Strategy*.* It was designed to earn 100% a year in a flat or up market. I decided to invest exclusively in the NASDAQ 100 tracking stock (QQQQ) to avoid the difficult decision of picking the right underlying stock.

By the end of the year, the account had grown in value to over $29,600, an incredible increase of over 196%.

Has anyone ever made 196% in a single year by writing covered calls? I don't think so. But every single person who followed my advice in 2003 made 196% with my *10K Strategy* (the same strategy I used, with a few tweaks, to make over 50% a year for the past several years in several portfolios at *Terry's Tips* using a variety of individual stocks and ETFs as the underlyings).

The *Mighty Mesa Strategy* is a modification of the *10K Strategy*. Instead of going for 100% a year, it aims at a lower return with a much higher likelihood of achieving that more reasonable goal every year.

---

* I called it the *10K Strategy* because it wasn't a sprint (like day-trading) nor was it a marathon (where you had to wait a very long time to see results).

Education is hanging around
until you've caught on.

— ROBERT FROST

CHAPTER 7

Calendar Spreads and Butterfly Spreads

Earlier, I said that I would ask you to understand only two kinds of option spreads — a calendar spread (also called a time spread) which is the most important part of the entire *Mighty Mesa Strategy*, and a butterfly spread which is used in this strategy to protect against a big move in the stock (usually on the downside).

First of all, an options spread is simply having two options, one which you buy (once you buy it, you are *long* that option) and one which you sell (once you sell it, you are *short* that option). When you buy a spread, you only have to come up with the difference in the prices of the two options.

Spreads can be either puts or calls, but one side of the spread can't be a put and the other side a call without incurring a margin requirement. The *Mighty Mesa Strategy* does not employ any spreads that require margin — that is why it can be conducted in an IRA account.

Calendar Spreads

Calendar spreads are the basic foundation of the *Mighty Mesa Strategy*. They involve buying an option that has several months of remaining life and simultaneously selling another option in the current month with both the long and short option having the same strike price. Since the longer-term option will always be more valuable than the short-term one, buying the spread will involve the outlay of some money (when you place the order, it is called a debit).

A typical order for a new calendar spread looks like this:

BTO (Buy To Open) 5 SPY Apr-09 87 calls
STO (Sell To Open) 5 SPY Dec-08 87 calls for a debit of $4.60

In this example, the Dec-08 87 call had one month of remaining life at the time of this order and was trading at $6.00 while the Apr-09 call with 5 months of remaining life was trading at $10.60. (This was

You can never learn less,
you can only learn more.

— R. BUCKMINSTER FULLER

an at-the-money spread since SPY was trading at $87 at this time.) In order to buy this calendar spread, you would have to pay $4.60 ($460) per spread, plus commissions.

The *Mighty Mesa Strategy* gains money because the short-term short option (Dec-08 87 call) will go down in value (decay) at a faster rate than the longer-term long option (Apr-09 87 call). In this example, the Dec-08 87 call will decay by $600 in one month while the average monthly decay of the Apr-09 87 call is $212 ($1060/5).

In the *Mighty Mesa Strategy*, once a calendar spread has been purchased, the normal procedure is to wait until the current-month short option is just about to expire, and then roll it over to the next month at the same strike. This is what a roll-over trade would like:

BTC (Buy to Close) 5 SPY Dec-08 87 calls
STO (Sell To Open) 5 SPY Jan-09 87 calls for a credit of $5.00

Since the Jan-09 87 call has a longer lifespan than the Dec-08 87 call which is about to expire, it is worth more, and the spread can be executed at a credit. In this example, the entire cost of the original spread ($460) is more than recouped with the roll-over sale ($500) and there will be three more opportunities to roll over the short-term call to the next month. The final roll-over will be a Sell to Close the Apr-09 87 call, and the spread will be gone.

Most brokers require you to tell them whether option trades you are placing are opening or closing positions, and it is often a pain in the neck to figure out. My broker, *thinkorswim*, does not require this information, and that is one of the many reasons I prefer them to other brokers.

Calendar spreads are the most profitable when the stock price is exactly at the strike price when the short-term short options expire. The further the stock moves from that strike price (in either direction), the less can be obtained from the roll-over trade. Since we have no idea of where the stock might end up at the next expiration, the *Mighty Mesa Strategy* involves buying calendar spreads at several dif-

People who never get
carried away should be.

— MALCOLM FORBES

ferent strike prices, some at strikes higher than the stock price (usually calls), and some at strikes below the stock price (usually puts).

We prefer calls for strikes above the stock price and puts for strikes below the stock price because they are more likely to be out of the money as expiration nears. This means there is less risk of an early exercise of the short option, and better roll-over prices are generally available when the options are not well in the money as expiration nears.

Appendix B discusses why the strike price is more important than whether the options are puts or calls in calendar spreads. At different times, the cost of a put calendar spread may be considerably more expensive than the same-strike call calendar spread (and at other times, the reverse could be true). When we place calendar spreads in the *Mighty Mesa Strategy*, we usually buy the least expensive spread available for the calendar spreads which are at strike prices very close to the stock price, regardless of whether they are puts or calls.

Butterfly Spreads

A butterfly spread is an interesting options tactic if you think you know where a stock will end up at expiration. Most people select a range of strike prices within which they believe the stock will end up, and use that range for the outer parameters of the spread.

Let's say that SPY is trading at $130 with a month to go until expiration. You believe that the stock will end up within a few dollars of the same price when it expires in 4 weeks. To set up a butterfly spread, you might buy one option at the 134 strike, sell two options at the 130 strike, and buy one option at the 126 strike. All of these options are for the current expiration month.

Most people use calls for butterfly spreads, but it really doesn't make any difference whether you use calls or puts. The mathematics are identical. The nearer the stock is to the mid-point of the range of strikes at expiration, the greater the gain. If the stock ends up outside the range of strikes, the spread expires worthless, and you lose everything you paid for the spread at the outset.

Live as if you were to die tomorrow.
Learn as if you were to live forever.

— MOHANDAS GANDHI

Here are the gain/loss possibilities for a long 1 134 — short 2 130 — long 1 126 option butterfly spread:

Stock Price at Expiration	Gain
Above $134	$ 0
$133	$100
$132	$200
$131	$300
$130	$400
$129	$300
$128	$200
$127	$100
Below $126	$ 0

With 4 weeks until expiration and SPY selling at about $130, this 134-130-126 butterfly would cost $120 to buy. In order for you to break even, the stock would have to end up above $127.20 and below $132.80 for you to cover the cost of the initial spread. If the stock ends up exactly at $130, the spread would be worth $400, or more than 3 times what you paid for it at the outset.

Many people like the 3-1 possible odds of a butterfly spread. In the real world, there is an additional little kicker that makes them like butterflies even more. If just before expiration, the stock is trading just outside the range of strikes (and if it expires at that price you will lose everything you paid for the spread), there will still be some good time premium remaining in the long option you own at the strike closest to the current stock price. With even a few hours before the options expire, you may be able to sell the spread for something, perhaps as much as half what you paid for it. So when the worst thing happens, sometimes you can recover some of your initial investment.

In the *Mighty Mesa Strategy* we do not buy butterfly spreads because we think we know where the stock will end up at expiration. In fact, **a basic assumption of the *Mighty Mesa Strategy* is that we have no idea where the stock will go in the short run.** Since we don't

Anyone who lives within their means
suffers from a lack of imagination.

— Oscar Wilde

have any idea about what it will do, we want to insure against the possibility that it might go up or down (if it stays the same, we know we will make good money — it's only when it moves too much that we encounter possible loss situations).

Even though we have no idea where the stock will end up, we buy butterfly spreads almost every month in the *Mighty Mesa* portfolios. We do it for insurance purposes, just in case the stock does move in the direction of a certain range of strike prices.

Usually, we buy butterfly spreads with a range of strike prices which are lower than the current stock price. As a rule of thumb, we select a range of strikes where the highest strike is just below the stock price and the mid-point of the range (where the two short options are) is about 5% below the stock price.

In the above example, we would buy a 128-124-120 butterfly spread when the stock was selling at $130. In order for us to make the maximum gain on this spread, the stock would have to fall all the way down to $124 (almost 5%).

The great thing about buying spreads at these strikes is that they are much cheaper. Instead of paying $120 for the 134-130-126 spread we could buy the 128-124-120 spread for only $60, or about half as much. Since the stock would have to fall by at least $2 at expiration before there would be any value to the spread, the market places a lower value on the lower-strikes spread.

If the stock does manage to fall by $6 at expiration, the spread we paid $60 for would be worth $400, or over 6 times what we paid for it. The insurance we had purchased would have paid off. Most of the time we expect that the cost of this insurance would not have any value at expiration, just like the premiums you might have paid for a traditional insurance policy.

In those instances when we collect on our butterfly spread insurance policy, if we had set up our positions correctly at the outset of the month, the gain on the butterfly spreads would cover the losses we incurred on the higher-strike calendar spreads that would have

You have to learn the rules of the game.
And then you have to play better
than anyone else.

— ALBERT EINSTEIN

made their biggest gains if the stock had remained flat or gone up moderately.

When we buy butterfly spreads which are below the stock price we use puts, and when they are at strikes above the stock price we use calls even though the mathematics of the pay-offs are the same. This tactic means that the absolute value of the options is less, and the bid-asked spreads are usually lower (meaning that we get better prices for the options we buy and sell).

Butterfly spreads are flexible instruments. You can choose a larger or smaller range of strikes if you wish. For example, you could buy a 135-130-125 range or a 140-130-120 range. The larger the range, the more expensive the spread will be.

There are also some interesting permutations that I have found effective at times, such as buying one option at the 128 strike, selling 3 options at the 124 strike and buying 2 options at the 122 strike (this spread would only cost $55 rather than $60 and would give you the same maximum profit point at the 124 strike).

Another variation that is used in the *Mighty Mesa Strategy* is to buy a longer-term option rather than the current month option at the highest-strike price in the above put butterfly spread. While this ties up more cash, the real cost of that option (which is the most expensive option in the butterfly spread) is the decay on the longer-term option rather than what you would have paid for the current-month option.

I don't want to unnecessarily complicate this discussion by bringing up some of the possible permutations of butterfly spreads, but if you are interested in becoming an option guru on your own, you might consider some of the alternatives you have at your disposal.

For most people, it would be far easier to become a *Terry's Tips* Insider and mirror (or just watch) the trades I make in the *Mighty Stalagmite* or the other *Mighty Mesa* portfolios or have those trades placed in your account automatically by your broker through his Auto-Trade program.

Every once in a while, the market
does something so stupid it
takes your breath away.

— JIM CRAMER

CHAPTER 8

Finding the Right Underlying

Stock options are derivatives. Their value is dependent upon or derived from one or more underlying assets (for our purposes, called the underlying). The derivative itself is merely a contract between two or more parties. Its value is primarily determined by fluctuations in the underlying asset.

Because derivatives are just contracts, just about anything can be used as an underlying asset, including stocks, bonds, commodities, currencies, interest rates and market indexes.

Most derivatives are characterized by high leverage. Derivatives got a bad name a few years back when a hedge fund called Long-Term Capital Management failed spectacularly in the late 1990s, leading to a massive bailout by other major banks and investment houses. Management of the fund included Nobel prize winners, and even they couldn't understand the implications of derivative. The fund lost $4.6 billion in 1998 in less than four months following the Russian financial crisis and became a prominent example of the risk potential in the hedge fund industry. The fund folded in early 2000.

The derivatives we are concerned with are rather tame compared to the exotic instruments that Long-Term Capital owned. Ours are based on fairly predicable underlyings — usually a tracking stock of a basket of companies — often called Exchange Traded Funds (ETFs).

While the *Mighty Mesa Strategy* can be used with the options of almost any underlying stock or ETF, there are important reasons why certain underlying stocks are far better than others.

As we have seen, the enemy of the *Mighty Mesa Strategy* is volatility. Since a large gain is always made if the stock stays absolutely flat, the best choice would seem to be a stock that just doesn't move very much. And for sure, there are a lot of them out there. We all have probably owned many of them over the years.

Some stocks do fluctuate a lot, such as Apple and Google, and option prices on these stocks are considerably higher than they are

I rarely think the market is right.
I believe non dividend stocks aren't
much more than baseball cards.
They are worth what you can
convince someone to pay for it.

— MARK CUBAN

for less volatile companies. However, when earnings announcements are made (or any of the other possible events mentioned in Chapter 2), the stock often surges or drops suddenly, and wipes out potential profits overnight.

The challenge is to find an underlying stock that has relatively high option premiums but is not subject to sudden price changes. The solution is not really a stock at all, but an Exchange Traded Fund (ETF) that is composed of a large number of different companies. The larger the number of companies in the ETF, the less likely a big stock price move will come about because of what happens to an individual company. However, the size of the companies in the ETF is also important — the Russell 2000 (IWM) which is made up of 2000 small-cap companies is more volatile than the Dow Jones Industrial Average tracking stock (DIA) which is made up of only 30 large companies.

Ultimately, the best underlying is a stock or ETF that fluctuates less than the Implied Volatility (IV) of the option prices. (IV is also called Projected Volatility which is probably a better term because it defines what the market is actually doing – projecting how much volatility that it expects). The only problem here is that there is no way of knowing in advance how much the underlying will fluctuate in the future.

You can get an idea of how much an underlying might fluctuate by checking out its historic volatility, but that is backward looking. The important thing is what will happen in the future, and as we have already quoted one great sage, "predictions are very difficult to make, especially when they involve the future."

Individual stocks are generally more volatile than ETFs, and option prices are typically higher for most individual stocks. As I write this, Apple is trading at about the same price as SPY, and a one-month at-the-money call on Apple trades at $9.50 compared to $6.30 for the same call on SPY.

Over the years, we have experimented with several different underlyings with mixed results. Google is a special case in itself. The com-

In this business if you're good,
you're right six times out of ten.
You're never going to be right
nine times out of ten.

— Peter Lynch

pany typically does not give much guidance to the investment community about what earnings will be, and this is cause for great uncertainty (and high option prices). Even more significant, they usually schedule their quarterly earnings announcements only one or two days before an option expiration date (the third Friday of the month). Just prior to that time, option prices go through the roof. An at-the-money put or call with only a single day of remaining life might trade for 5% or more of the price of the stock since that is how much the market anticipates the stock might move once the announcement is made.

For a couple of years, we ran a Google portfolio at *Terry's Tips* with interesting results. We usually did pretty well in the two out of three months that did not include an earnings announcement, but in that third month, the stock was so turbulent (often more than 5% on a single day) that we lost everything (or more) than we had gained in the other two months. We closed down the portfolio because of the huge monthly swings in value even though we had made some decent gains over the entire lifetime of the portfolio.

A similar situation occurred with Apple. For two years in a row, we gained over 100% for the year in our Apple portfolio. However, in less than half a year, it climbed from $90 to $180. This wasn't so bad because we started out each month with a bullish stance, but large swings in the stock price hurt portfolio values even if they are in the direction you are betting.

When Apple fell from $180 back to $90 in less than three months our portfolio got clobbered, and we decided to no longer use Apple or any other individual stocks as the underlyings.

You might wonder why we didn't choose a company that didn't fluctuate much in price for underlying instead of a company as volatile as Google or Apple. The answer is simple. The problem with such stable stocks is that the market recognizes that they don't fluctuate much, and the option prices are dreadfully low, so low that the strategy just doesn't work.

I hate weekends because
there is no stock market.

— RENE RIVKIN

Some ETFs fluctuate nearly as much as individual stocks. In 2004, we suffered large losses in the NASDAQ 100 tracking stock (QQQQ) when this stock simply fluctuated far more than the option prices could tolerate. We have continued to follow QQQQ over the years since that time, and it continues to follow the same pattern.

We have concluded that QQQQ is not a suitable underlying for our strategy. In fact, we suspect better gains could have been made by buying short-term options on QQQQ rather than selling them as our strategy dictates. But buying options in not our game, and we will leave it to others who are smarter or luckier than we are to play.

Another ETF that did not work out because of excessive volatility was the Emerging Markets ETF (EEM) which consists of larger companies in over 20 emerging countries with a concentration in BRIC (Brazil, Russia, India, and China). We thought that adding a portfolio based on Emerging Markets would provide some international diversification from the domestic nature of our other portfolios, but we were reminded that volatility is the major enemy, and not the direction of the price changes.

After kicking the tires of many ETFs over the years, we have settled on four favorites. The most conservative (and the one we have done the best with) is the S&P 500 (SPY), followed by the Dow Jones Industrial Average tracking stock (DIA) which has also proved to be consistently profitable.

The other two ETFs we use are more volatile (and have higher option prices as well, which means than in flat markets they should do better than SPY or DIA, but in volatile markets they should do worse (as has been our experience).

The Russell 2000 (small cap) Index (IWM), started in 1984, is a subset of the larger Russell 3000. It is one of the most widely used indexes by investors and is generally accepted as the benchmark for small-cap firms. It includes many newer, smaller firms that are not represented by the S&P 500 or other large indexes.

Though the index contains smaller, more volatile companies, the Russell 2000 has handily outperformed its large-cap peers since its

*There are two times in a man's life
when he should not speculate:
when he can't afford it, and when he can.*

— MARK TWAIN

inception. It trades more shares than all the other Russell ETFs put together.

SPY, DIA, and IWM have many characteristics that make them particularly attractive as underlyings. The options are actively traded and quite liquid, and strikes are available at every dollar increment so we can fine-tune our risk level more precisely than for other stocks or ETFs that might only trade at $5 increments for the higher strike prices There are small differences between bid and asked prices for the options, so you don't pay a huge transaction cost when buying or selling.

Another advantage of these three ETFs is that starting in 2008, quarterly options that expire at or near the end of the month are available in December, March, June, and September in addition to the regular option series for those months that expire on the third Friday. Since the *Mighty Mesa Strategy* usually makes the greatest gains in the last few days of an expiration period, these quarterly options provide four extra opportunities for maximum gains each year.

The final ETF used at *Terry's Tips* is the most volatile one, and was set up because it often moved in the opposite direction of the broad-market based ETFs. It is the Oil Services ETF (OIH) which is a narrow-based index made up of only 18 companies in the same industry. OIH options have high premiums because volatility is high, and this ETF often behaves more like an individual (and volatile) stock rather than an ETF. OIH options are only available at increments which are $5 apart up to $200 where they are $10 apart, and quarterly options are not offered. In spite of these shortcomings, we have continued to offer a portfolio using OIH as the underlying because it offers a degree of diversification and often does better than the other portfolios in months when the market is flat.

One way to end up with $1 million
is to start with $2 million
and use technical analysis.

— RALPH SEGER

CHAPTER 9

An Options Strategy
that Never* Loses Money

In this chapter I will discuss the asterisk after the word "Never." I can make the statement that the *Mighty Mesa Strategy* never* loses money based on two sets of numbers. First, the following risk profile graph shows how much money a portfolio of SPY options will gain or lose in a one-month period at a range of possible prices for the underlying SPY stock.

Second, I check back on how much SPY has fluctuated each expiration month for the past 10 years (those numbers are summarized later). By comparing the graph and the table of SPY monthly fluctuations I could determine the loss or gain that would have resulted each month during those 10 years.

A third variable is not as easily measured but is an important part of the strategy. It consists of making an adjustment to the portfolio when the stock has fluctuated dangerously close to a point where a loss situation might be encountered. We will discuss that near the end of this chapter.

I spend time every trading day studying a graph similar to this for each of the (currently seven) option portfolios I manage. Each week,

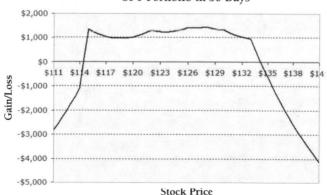

SPY Portfolio in 30 Days

105

Money can't buy happiness,
but it can buy you the kind
of misery you prefer.

— AUTHOR UNKNOWN

I publish an updated graph for each portfolio for *Terry's Tips* sub-scribers so they can see their potential gains or losses for the current month at a variety of possible stock prices.

The portfolio of SPY options on page 105 was set up at the begin-ning of the August 2008 expiration month with $10,000 when SPY was trading at $124. (In the next chapter, I will explain which specific options were used to create this graph, and how you can create a similar graph on your own.)

The graph shows that the portfolio will gain about 10% (before commissions) in one month if SPY ends up at any price on expiration Friday between $115 and $133. In other words, the stock can fall by $9 (7.2%) or go up by $9 (7.2%) and a 10% gain will result.

Of course, if the stock moves beyond those limits in 30 days, losses will accrue which are much greater than 10%. An important part of a prudent options strategy would be to provide some protection for the portfolio when the stock moved to either end of the break-even profit range of $115 to $133.

I invite you to compare these possible results where the stock price changes only moderately with any stock market investment you could come up with. If the stock stays flat or moves by less than 7% in a single month, the portfolio would make a profit of 10%.

How could anyone look at this graph and ever think that buying stock is safer than an options portfolio configured as this one is? For me, it is one of the great mysteries of the investment world, rank-ing right up there with why so many people buy non-index mutual funds. I just don't understand why supposedly intelligent adults make such bad investment decisions like this, year in and year out.

The 10-Year Backtest

Once the above graph has been created, the next step is to determine how much of the time that SPY manages to trade inside the break-even profit range of +/- 7.2%. This would be an easy task if all we had to do was calculate the percentage monthly changes that the stock

Money is better than poverty,
if only for financial reasons.

— Woody Allen

had made over the past 10 years.

Here are those fluctuation numbers for each expiration month (expiration months are either 4-week or 5-week periods ending on the 3rd Friday of each calendar month, and therefore not exactly the same as calendar month fluctuations):

	1999	2000	2001	2002	2003	2004	2005	2006	2007	2008
Jan	4.3%	1.2%	2.3%	-1.5%	1.2%	5.0%	-2.5%	-0.6%	0.2%	-11.3%
Feb	-0.8%	6.3%	-2.7%	-2.5%	-6.3%	0.3%	2.8%	2.1%	1.9%	6.2%
Mar	4.2%	8.6%	-11.8%	5.9%	5.6%	-3.6%	-1.1%	1.2%	-4.8%	-3.4%
Apr	1.1%	-2.1%	8.3%	-3.6%	1.7%	3.0%	-3.8%	0.4%	6.7%	3.9%
May	0.5%	-1.9%	4.2%	-1.3%	-0.4%	-3.3%	4.4%	2.9%	2.9%	3.2%
June	0.4%	3.9%	-6.1%	-10.3%	5.6%	2.8%	1.8%	-1.3%	0.3%	-7.9%
July	5.6%	0.8%	-0.4%	14.1%	0.1%	-2.7%	1.5%	-1.2%	0.1%	-2.7%
Aug	0.6%	1.4%	-3.8%	10.8%	0.2%	-0.2%	0.0%	5.0%	-6.1%	3.3%
Sept	-0.1%	-2.5%	-16.7%	-9.7%	3.7%	2.4%	0.8%	1.4%	4.7%	-4.8%
Oct	-6.6%	-4.2%	10.4%	6.0%	1.4%	-1.3%	-4.3%	3.8%	-1.8%	-25.1%
Nov	14.1%	-2.3%	6.5%	3.7%	-0.2%	5.9%	5.6%	2.8%	-2.1%	-16.6%
Dec	0.2%	-4.1%	0.5%	-2.3%	4.0%	1.9%	1.0%	1.5%	2.0%	

SPY changed by 7.2% in a single expiration month only 14 times in the past 10 years according to this table. Four of those months occurred consecutively in 2002, and three others occurred in 2008. While I don't want to get technical at this point, when the stock is as volatile as it was in 2002 and in late 2008, option prices become much higher. A risk profile graph created with those elevated option prices would have a much wider break-even profit range than the graph presented above with August 2008 option prices.

From 2003 through 2007, a period of 5 years, SPY did not fluctuate more than 7.2% in either direction in a single expiration month. It is easy to understand why the actual portfolios at *Terry's Tips* made average gains of over 50% during that entire period (except in 2004 when unusual mid-month whip-saw price activity and 9-year low option prices conspired to cause losses — this was before the current

Inflation hasn't ruined everything.
A dime can still be used as a screwdriver.

— QUOTED IN P.S. I LOVE YOU,
COMPILED BY H. JACKSON BROWN, JR.

strategy with downside insurance protection had been established).

If we only looked at the monthly fluctuations in the stock price you might conclude that the portfolio would make money 86% of the time, and that the average profit might be about 7% or 8% (taking commissions and roll-over transaction costs into consideration). Unfortunately, this would be an overly-optimistic assessment of the profit possibilities of the *Mighty Mesa Strategy.*

A more realistic approach would recognize the dangerous position that the portfolio gets into when one end of the break-even profit range is approached. Huge losses can result if the stock moves outside that range. If you happen to be in one of those months like October 2008 when the stock fell more 25% (which happened only once in the past 80 years), you might lose your profits for the past year in a single month.

When one end of the break-even profit range is approached, you can't just sit there and do nothing, hoping the stock won't keep moving in that same direction. If you are wrong, all your wonderful gains for the past year or so might disappear in one ugly week.

I call the price when action must be taken the *Shoulder Price.* In the above risk profile graph, it occurs at $115 and $133. If you were on a land formation shaped like the graph, at those prices you would be looking over the edge of a cliff and in great danger. You can't just hang on and hope you don't fall off and get killed.

When that *Shoulder Price* is approached, insurance must be purchased that will protect against a further price movement in that same direction (the risk profile graph shows that you are equally exposed on the upside as you are on the downside). The price of the insurance policy will understandably reduce or eliminate the gains that you hoped to make in that month.

In proclaiming that the *Mighty Mesa Strategy* never* loses money, I am assuming that it can avoid a big loss in those months when insurance must be purchased to protect against a further change in the stock price.

Insurance may come in the form of using any spare cash in the

Wealth — any income that is at least
one hundred dollars more a year
than the income of one's wife's
sister's husband.

— H.L. Mencken

portfolio to buy a new a butterfly spread or taking off calendar spreads at the other end of the original graph range and replacing them with spreads at strikes in the direction that the stock has moved (Chapter 11 explains how to make these insurance adjustments.)

How often will insurance adjustments need to be made (telling us also how many months can be expected to end up with no meaning-ful gains)? In order to answer this question, rather than looking at the actual percentage change in the stock, we need to examine how often the stock moved by a sufficiently large enough amount to trigger an insurance adjustment.

If a stock fell by 9% at some time during the month but then went back up so that the actual change for the month was 6%, the portfolio would enjoy a big gain for the month if we had done nothing, but we couldn't take the chance that it might not stay down 9% or go even further (either possibility would cause losses).

We need to calculate the number of expiration months that the stock price changes mid-month by an amount that would trigger an insurance adjustment. As a rule of thumb, I have set the limit at 6%. If the stock moves by 6% in either direction, an adjustment is in order. This trigger number is well below the *Shoulder Price* numbers which are 7.2% away from the starting price of SPY in the above example.

In the table on page 115 are the actual results for the last ten years, comparing the starting price of the stock going into the expiration month with the highest (and lowest) price it hit during the month:

I find it interesting that the stock changed by 5% in an expiration month exactly the same number of times (29) on the upside as it did on the downside, but the big changes (10% or more) were almost all on the downside.

The stock went up by more than 10% only 4 times in 10 years, and 2 of those months occurred back in the go-go year of 1998 and 1999. On the downside, however, it fell by 10% more than an average of once a year (12 double-digit drops over 10 years).

Because big drops are three times as likely to be on the downside as they are on the upside, the *Mighty Mesa Strategy* provides for butterfly

All I ask is the chance to prove that
money can't make me happy.

— Spike Milligan

#	Month	Largest Gain	Ending Change	Month	Largest Loss	Ending Change
1	Nov-99	14.5%	14.1%	Oct-08	-32.8%	-25.1%
2	Aug-02	11.9%	10.8%	Nov-08	-22.0%	-16.6%
3	Oct-01	11.5%	7.7%	Sep-01	-19.7%	-16.7%
4	Nov-98	10.1%	10.0%	Jul-02	-14.5%	-14.1%
5	Feb-08	9.7%	6.2%	Sep-98	-13.8%	-6.0%
6	Mar-00	9.5%	8.7%	Mar-01	-12.4%	-12.2%
7	Apr-01	8.8%	7.6%	Jan-08	-11.9%	-11.3%
8	Jun-03	8.5%	5.6%	Aug 07	-11.1%	-6.1%
9	Jan-99	7.8%	4.3%	Oct-00	-11.1%	-4.4%
10	Nov-01	7.5%	6.6%	Jun-02	-11.0%	-10.3%
11	Nov-04	7.4%	5.9%	Feb-03	-10.9%	-6.3%
12	Mar-02	7.0%	5.9%	Sep-02	-10.1%	-9.7%
13	Dec-02	6.8%	6.0%	Oct-98	-9.7%	3.8%
14	Apr-07	6.7%	6.7%	Apr-00	-9.1%	-2.1%
15	Mar-99	6.6%	4.2%	Jul 08	-8.8%	-2.7%
16	Sep-07	6.4%	4.7%	Jun-08	-8.1%	-7.9%
17	Apr-00	6.0%	-2.1%	Dec-02	-7.9%	6.0%
18	Jul-99	5.8%	5.6%	Mar 08	-7.8%	-3.4%
19	Mar-03	5.8%	5.6%	Feb-00	-7.6%	-7.1%
20	Nov-08	5.8%	-16.6%	Jun-01	-7.3%	-6.2%
21	Nov-05	5.8%	5.6%	Oct-99	-6.9%	-6.6%
22	Nov-02	5.6%	3.7%	May-02	-6.7%	-1.3%
23	Jun-00	5.6%	3.8%	Mar-03	-6.5%	5.6%
24	Dec-07	5.2%	2.0%	Mar-07	-6.1%	-4.8%
25	May-01	5.2%	4.9%	Apr-02	-6.0%	-3.6%
26	May-00	5.1%	-0.3%	May-03	-5.6%	-0.4%
27	Jan-04	5.1%	5.0%	Apr-01	-5.6%	7.6%
28	Oct-98	5.1%	3.8%	Oct-05	-5.3%	-4.3%
29	Aug-06	5.0%	5.0%	Feb-02	-5.1%	-2.5%
30	Apr-99	4.9%	1.1%	Jan-01	-4.9%	1.5%

Every day I get up and look through
the Forbes list of the richest people
in America. If I'm not there, I go to work.

— ROBERT ORBEN

spreads at the outset on the downside but not on the upside. Most of the time, these butterfly spreads are expected to expire worthless so that the portfolio loses the entire amount that those spreads originally cost. For this reason, it is generally best to refrain from buying butterfly spreads for upside protection at the outset (an interesting feature of butterfly spreads is that they do not get appreciably more expensive as expiration is approached, so it is possible to postpone their purchase without risking adverse prices later on).

The table shows that in almost half the months when the stock rises by 6% sometimes during the month, it ends up that month with a smaller gain than 6%. For this reason, it is best to be a little slow to make upside insurance adjustments (remember, these adjustments cost money and may mean that no gains are made in the months when adjustments are made).

Three times in the 10-year period, the stock rose by 6% in a single month and also fell by 6% sometime during that same month (April 2000, April 2001, and December 2002). The *Mighty Mesa Strategy* would surely have lost money during those 3 times in 120 months, but the losses should not have been too great because the stock ended outside the shoulder price limits only once, and that was by a very small margin.

Almost always, a double-digit change in the price of SPY was followed by a change in the opposite direction in the following month. Except for two occasions in 1998 and 1999 when the Internet-inspired bubble was pushing stocks up by huge margins every month, and in October–November 2008, this was the case.

In carrying out the *Mighty Mesa Strategy*, we take the position that we have no idea which way the stock price will move in the next month. The only exception to this policy is in those rare months when a double-digit change in stock price comes along – when we set up the positions for the next month we would "lean" in the direction of the expected change, setting the mid-point of the risk profile graph a little higher or lower than the current stock price, depending on the

*The only thing we know for certain
about technical analysis is that it's
possible to make a living publishing
a newsletter on the subject.*

— Martin S. Fridson,
Investment Illusions

direction of the prior month's double-digit change.

When we set up the *Mighty Mesa Strategy* portfolios at the beginning of the November 2008 expiration month, since SPY had fallen sharply (over 25%) in October, we expected higher prices in November, and we established positions that would do best if the stock rose. When SPY fell again (by 16.6%) in November, we were still able to make gains in our SPY portfolios because the extreme market volatility had pushed options price sharply higher which allowed the strategy to tolerate larger than normal price fluctuations.

Proof that This Strategy Never* Loses Money?

The asterisk after the word "Never" refers to the qualification that the claim is made based on a 10-year backtest of the volatility of SPY. What do these numbers tell us?

First, insurance adjustments would have had to be made in 17 out of 120 months when the stock rose by 6% at some point during the month, and in 25 months when the stock fell by 6% at some point during the month. That works out to a total of 42 months out of 120, or about 35% of the time when an adjustment would be necessary.

I have assumed that on balance, these months would result in no gain for the month. Some months will show a small loss and others would show a small gain, but on balance, I am projecting break-even results for those months.

The leap of faith you must take here is to accept the claim that the insurance policy (the new butterfly spread) can be purchased for a sufficiently low price so that the portfolio will not lose money in those months when insurance needs to be bought.

Unfortunately, it is impossible to tell in advance the exact cost of the downside insurance adjustments. My 30 years of option trading experience tell me that the cost will be low enough to assure us that we will not lose money in most of the months when adjustments become necessary.

I could say "Trust me, I am a doctor," but we both know that is not enough. You need more evidence. The first thing I can offer is for you

Technical analysts are the witch doctors
of our business. By deciphering stock price
movement patterns and volume changes,
these Merlins believe they can
forecast the future.

— WILLIAM GROSS,
EVERYTHING YOU'VE HEARD ABOUT INVESTING IS WRONG!

to check out the Track Record on my website — **www.TerrysTips. com/TrackRecord** for the latest update on how the several actual portfolios performed when adjustments needed to be made.

Over time, we will gain a better understanding of the costs of the insurance adjustments. A lot of the cost will ultimately be determined by the timing of the drop (or advance) of the stock during the expiration month. I do encourage you to check the Track Record page for a current report.

In the 65% of the months when no insurance adjustments would be necessary, the average gains in the portfolio might be about 7% (although we have recorded considerably higher monthly gains in our actual *Mighty Mesa* portfolios). While the risk profile graph shows 10% average possible gains, that number should be reduced by at least 3% to account for commission costs and the bid-asked spread penalty when rolling over options from one month to the next.

If a portfolio gained 7% after commissions in 65% of the months while breaking even in the other 35% of the months, the annual gain would work out to be a whopping 55%. That is probably an overly optimistic number. I feel much more comfortable saying that the *Mighty Mesa Strategy* might gain 36% consistently every year, year in and year out. I suspect most investors would be delighted with those kinds of results.

Early experience in the actual portfolios suggests that it might be possible to do better than break even in the volatile months when adjustments need to be made. In the portfolio using the Dow Jones Industrial Average tracking stock (DIA), the first four months recorded an average 7.5% monthly gain after commissions even though two of these months (October and November) had greater volatility than the market had had in several decades. Three SPY portfolios (one bullish, one bearish, and one ultra-conservative) gained an average of 1% per month after commissions through the difficult October-November 2008 extreme volatility months when several adjustments had to be made.

Part III

$

PUTTING the MIGHTY MESA STRATEGY to WORK

Try a thing you haven't done three times.
Once, to get over the fear of doing it.
Twice, to learn how not to do it.
And a third time to figure out
whether you like it or not.

— Virgil Thomson

CHAPTER 10
Setting Up A Mighty Mesa

There are two ways you can determine the best positions for a successful *Mighty Mesa* portfolio. The easiest way would be to subscribe to *Terry's Tips* and let me do it for you. The other way is to do it yourself, and this chapter will spell out exactly what I do so you can accomplish it on your own if you wish.

Creating a *Mighty Mesa* portfolio involves going through a series of what-if scenarios using one of two software packages. The first one is available free for clients at *thinkorswim* – it is the Analyze Tab on their trading platform. Once you're on that page, enter the underlying symbol in the upper left-hand box, change the P/L OPEN drop-down to P/L DAY, and move the date in the lower left-hand corner to one day after the next expiration date. Then click on the ADD SIMULATED TRADES tab, and enter the trades you want as if you were actually placing orders. After entering the spreads you want, go to the RISK PROFILE tab to see the results for those positions.

The second software package is an Excel program that I used to generate the graphs in this book. It was developed by a young man named Kai Reinke who lives in Argentina and only costs $37.90. As a special offer, readers of this book can order it at **http://www.kainini-to.com/optioncalculator** with a $5 discount — for a total cost of only $32.90. (I have recommended him so often that he offers a discount to people I send along).

I use both sets of software whenever I am creating a *Mighty Mesa* portfolio because they sometimes result in slightly different curves (for some strange reason I have not be able to fathom), and as a test to make certain I did not make an input error.

This Excel software package does everything I want and more, and most of all, is easy to use. What I like best about it is that once you enter your positions, you click an update button, the current market

Success is often just an idea away.

— FRANK TYGER

prices are looked up for you, and the graph updated. There is a complete user manual at the MISC tab just in case you have questions.

I use both sets of software every day to monitor my positions as the month unfolds, but the most important time is at the beginning of an expiration month when I enter what-if scenarios and see where those positions will leave me.

Let's use the S&P 500 tracking stock SPY as an example, setting up a $10,000 *Mighty Mesa* portfolio 30 days before an expiration when the stock is trading at $123. The goal is to create a risk profile graph which shows a relatively fixed gain for the portfolio if the stock were to close at any point between $113 and $133 in 30 days.

In other words, I want to be in a position where I don't care which way the stock goes as long as it doesn't fluctuate more than 8% in either direction. I would like to make the same gain at any price within a $20 range of possible stock prices. (For ETFs which are more volatile than SPY, I would select a range that is greater than 8% in either direction).

The first thing I do is enter some calendar spreads which are at strikes both below and above the $123 stock price, and use up about $7500 of the proposed portfolio. In this example, I bought options which had four months of remaining life for the long positions, and sold the current month (30 days of remaining life) against them.

Generally, I prefer to buy *put* calendar spreads at strike prices below the stock price and *call* calendar spreads at strikes above the stock price, although the risk profile graph is the same regardless of whether puts or calls are used (see Appendix B). The reason for this preference is that it is easier to trade out-of-the-money options than in-the-money options (bid-asked spreads tend to be smaller and the options are generally more liquid for out-of-the-money options).

In the following example, I bought *call* calendar spreads at the 122 strike even though that was a strike below the strike price because they were cheaper than the put prices at the time. (When market sentiment is negative, call spreads are usually cheaper than put spreads, and vice versa). The 122 strike was so close to the stock price that I

You can never be too rich or too thin.

— Duchess of Windsor

wasn't worried about it becoming too much in the money in the first month so I could select the least expensive spread available at that strike.

I entered 4 calendar spreads at each of these strikes: 120, 122, 124, and 126. This is what the risk profile graph looked like with these four spreads:

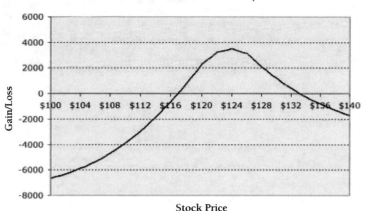

SPY Portfolio in 30 Days

This graph is typical of those which we used at *Terry's Tips* when we were seeking 50%–100% annual gains with what we called the *10K Strategy*. An extremely high gain would result if the stock ended up within a dollar or two of the starting price of $123, and would gain less as the stock moved away from that point.

The break-even (B/E) range is $117–$133, just a little less than the $20 range I am seeking. However, the graph looks much more like a mountain than it does a mesa — I don't make much money at all if the stock falls by $5. With these positions, I really need a flat market for the next 30 days in order to make a decent gain.

It is important to understand that when you own calendar spreads, you make the greatest gain when the stock ends up at expiration exactly at the strike price of your spread. When calendar spreads are

Don't play for safety — it's the most
dangerous thing in the world.

— HUGH WALPOLE

purchased at several different strike prices, you increase your chances of having the stock end up very close to one of those strike prices.

It is interesting to note that while an equal number of calendar spreads were placed at strikes below the stock price and above it, the portfolio will gain more if the stock moves higher. There is a bullish bias to call calendar spreads (and three of four of the spreads employ calls). While it is a slight bias, it should be recognized.

In the above graph, I can see that I need more protection at lower strikes. In the *Mighty Mesa* strategy, we use put butterfly spreads to provide that protection. First, we will see what the graph looks like if we used our remaining $2500 to buy 12 butterfly spreads at the 120-116-112 strikes (we buy 12 puts at the 120 strike, sell 24 puts at the 116 strike, and buy 12 puts at the 112 strike).

Instead of using the current month for all three options of the spread, we will go out an extra month for the long 120 strike put. While this ties up a little more cash, it considerably reduces the real cost of the butterfly spread because the ultimate cost will be the decay of that put for 30 days rather than the entire cost of a one-month 120 put.

If the stock were to end up at exactly at $120, a traditional butterfly spread (all options in the same month) would end up worthless. However, our modified butterfly spread would make a nice profit (all the current month options would expire worthless but our remaining 120 put with 30 days of remaining life would have about doubled in value).

On page 133 is what the graph looks like once the 12 butterfly spreads have been placed.

The B/E range has changed to $114–$130. This is the same 16-point range we had before placing the butterfly spreads, but it has moved down $3 at each end of the range.

The maximum potential profit is a whopping 40% if the stock were to end up anywhere between $117 and $125. Some people might be happy with this risk profile graph and stop here, but we want to spread our risk over a larger range of possible stock prices, even

*As for the Future, your task is not
to foresee but to enable it.*

— Antoine De Saint-Exupery

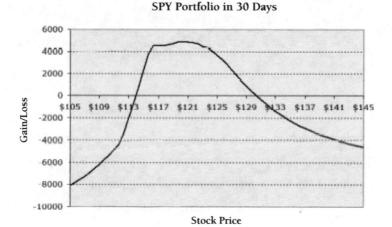

SPY Portfolio in 30 Days

though we will be giving up this huge potential gain within that 8-point range.

I would like to expand the downside B/E to $113 and increase the upside B/E price to $133 so I can achieve my objective of having $10 coverage in both directions. I can expand the downside number by lowering the strikes of the butterfly spread to 119-115-111 (and reducing the number to 10 spreads to generate a little cash).

To expand the upside B/E number, I will add 5 call calendar spreads at the 128 strike. In order to create cash for this new spread, I will have to reduce the number of call calendar spreads at the 120, 122, 124, 126 strikes from 4 each to 3 each.

The risk profile graph on page 135 looks like this with these new positions.

The shape of the graph is beginning to look a little more like a mesa, but there is still a big hump centered around the current $123 price, and the B/E range is still about a dollar short at either end of the range.

I can expand the downside B/E number by lowering the strikes of the put butterfly spread to 118-114-110 (and since it will be less

From birth to age 18, a girl needs good parents,
from 18 to 35 she needs good looks,
from 35 to 55 she needs a good personality,
and from 55 on she needs cash.

— Sophie Tucker

SPY Portfolio in 30 Days

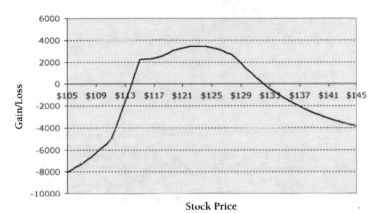

expensive to buy this spread, I can increase the number of spreads from 10 to 12).

On the upside, I will add 5 new calendar spreads at the 132 strike. In order to generate cash for these spreads, I will reduce the number lower-strike call calendar spreads so that I will have 2 at the 122, 124, 126 and 128 strikes, 4 at the 120 strike, and 3 at the 130 strike.

This is what the new risk profile graph looks like:

SPY Portfolio in 30 Days

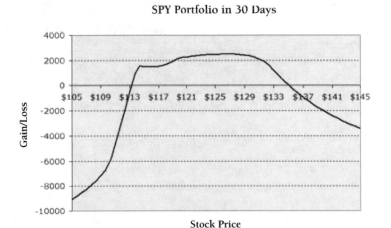

Rise early. Work hard. Strike oil.

— J. PAUL GETTY

Sleep late. Save a little.
Create a Mighty Mesa *portfolio.*

— TERRY ALLEN

The curve is surely looking more like a mesa than it does a mountain. I may have over-achieved on the upside since the B/E price is $135 rather than my goal of $133. Since I was feeling a little bullish this month, I decided to leave the extra protection on the upside. If I had wanted to move that number to $133, I could have reduced the number of 132 strike calendars and increased the number of lower-strike calendar spreads.

I am still a little concerned that at $113 we will only break even, and I would like to make a profit if the stock were to fall $10. I can achieve this by lowering the strikes of the modified put butterfly spread to 117-113-109 (and increasing the number of spreads to 13).

There is still a little hump in the graph around the $126 price, and I would like to keep a little cash in reserve, so I will reduce the number of 126 call calendar spreads to one, and come up with a new risk profile graph:

SPY Portfolio in 30 Days

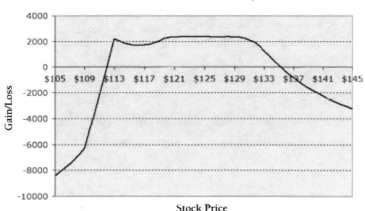

This is a graph I can live with. It looks like a mesa. I will make about a 20% gain (before commissions) if the stock were to land anywhere between $113 and $133 at expiration. I have a little cash set aside if I need it to expand the range of possible stock prices at either end of the spectrum.

We all covet wealth, but not its perils.

— JEAN DE LA BRUYERE

The final number of spreads for this *Mighty Mesa* portfolio are:

Calendar spreads (long side has four months of remaining life, short side has one month of remaining life):

4 puts at 120 strike
2 calls at 122 strike
2 calls at 124 strike
1 calls at 126 strike
2 calls at 128 strike
3 calls at 130 strike
5 calls at 132 strike

Butterfly Spreads: 13 long puts at highest strike(117) have two months of remaining life, 26 short puts (113) have one month of remaining life, and 13 long puts at lowest strike (109) have one month of remaining life.

I am not certain if this is the perfect selection of positions. Maybe I should have bought spreads at the odd-number strikes and reduced the numbers at the even-number strikes. If I wanted a larger B/E range and was willing to accept a lower gain across that larger range, I could lower the strikes of the put butterfly spread and add new call calendar spreads at even higher strikes (reducing the number of call calendar spreads at lower strikes).

In some portfolios, we are experimenting with using modified butterfly spreads with calls to expand the upside B/E range instead of using the highest-strike calendar spreads. At this point, our preference is for the calendar spreads since the market does manage to go up most of the time, so those spreads may become more valuable in future months.

Here are some general rules of thumb to set up a *Mighty Mesa* portfolio:

1. Calculate the desired break-even range of possible stock prices (for SPY, we recommend about 8% in either direction from the stock price).

The great rule is not to talk about money
with people who have much more or
much less than you.

— KATHERINE WHITEHORN

2. Place a small number of calendar spreads (2–5 months of remaining life for the long side, one month of remaining life for the short side) at strikes just below and above of the starting stock price. Long side options which only have 2 months of remaining life should only be bought when there is an extra quarterly option series available so that at least two sales of current-month options can be made.

3. Use puts for the calendar spreads below the stock price and calls for calendar spreads at strikes above the stock price unless there is a price advantage for those closest to the stock price. (In other words, if the call calendar spreads are less expensive, they can be used for strikes slightly below the stock price).

4. Place a larger number of calendar spreads at a strike approximately half-way between the stock price and the lowest strike in the break-even range that you have previously selected.

5. Place an even larger number of calendar spreads at the same strike as the upper end of the break-even range that you previously selected.

6. Place a put butterfly spread with the mid-point short puts at a strike which is the same as the downside break-even range end point (this spread will create the "shoulder" on the left side of the risk profile graph curve). The number of spreads should be at least double or triple the average number of calendar spreads that are placed at the various higher strikes.

7. Save some cash (maybe 5% of portfolio value) for future adjustments that might become necessary if the stock fluctuates more than usual. (For our most conservative portfolio, we set aside 10% of portfolio value for possible adjustments.)

These are just general guidelines. The real test of what works will show up in the risk profile graph you create.

You can see that it is not really difficult to set up a *Mighty Mesa* portfolio. It just takes a lot of experimenting until you get the curve that looks like a mesa and the shoulder at either end is just about

Life is either a daring adventure or nothing.
Security does not exist in nature,
nor do the children of men as a whole
experience it. Avoiding danger is not safer
in the long run than exposure.
— Helen Keller

where you would like it to be, given the likely volatility of the under-lying and your outlook for the market.

When deciding how many spreads to put on, it is important to remember that when you first set up a portfolio, your total account value falls immediately (by about 3% to 5%) because of the bid-asked-spread-penalty. This is usually overcome within a couple of weeks when the decay advantage has had some time to do its thing.

Once the *Mighty Mesa* portfolio has been set up, the same graphing software packages can be used to monitor the portfolio, and used as a basis for making the adjustments we will discuss in the next chapter.

*The road to success is usually
off the beaten path.*

— FRANK TYGER

CHAPTER 11
Making Adjustments

Once the original positions are established in the *Mighty Mesa Strategy*, adjustments are required every month. Roll-over trades generally occur just before the current month short options are about to expire. There are three kinds of roll-over trades (listed here by their frequency of occurring, from highest to lowest):

1. Current-month about-to-expire options are bought back and the same-strike options for the next month are sold.
2. Current-month about-to-expire options are bought back and the long options covering those current-month options are sold, thus taking off the calendar spread.
3. Current-month about-to-expire options are bought back and replaced by short options for the next month at a different strike price.

We employ two Trading Rules that call for buying back short options earlier than expiration week - the Average Daily Decay Calculation Rule, and the 8% Rule.

The average daily decay calculation Trading Rule generally becomes relevant for spreads at strikes which are furthest from the stock price (if the stock has fallen during the month, the highest-strike calendar spread will need to be checked, and if the stock has gone up during the month, the lowest-strike calendar spread will need watching).

This Trading Rule involves dividing the option price of the current month short option by the number of remaining days in its life, and comparing this calculation to the next-month same-strike option price divided by the number of days in its remaining life.

When the average daily decay of the current month option (the asked price) is less than the average daily decay of the next-month same-strike option (the bid price), it is time to buy back the current-month option.

Ideas are a commodity.
Execution of them is not.
— MICHAEL DELL

For example, if there are 10 days remaining until the September expiration (and 38 days until the October expiration) and you are short a September 72 option (bid $.05 — asked $.10), you would calculate the average daily decay by dividing $10 ($.10 x 100) by the number of remaining days (10) to get $1.00. (The *asked* price is used because you would have to buy back that option if you were to roll over to the next month.)

If the October 72 option is bid $.50 — asked $.60, the average daily decay would be $50/38 days, or $1.31. Since $1.31 is greater than $1.00, it would be time to buy back the short September 72 option. (For the October option, you would use the *bid* price because you would sell it if you were rolling over from September to October.)

Most of the time, when the average daily decay calculation comparison triggers a buy-back trade, the next-month same-strike option is sold at the same time. In the above example, this trade would be made:

BTC (Buy To Close) 5 XYZ Oct-08 72 calls
STO (Sell To Open) 5 XYZ Sep-08 72 calls for a credit of $1.20
— (selling a calendar)

However, before this trade is made, the current risk profile graph must be examined. Instead of selling the same-strike next month option, a better choice might be to sell an option at a different strike. This choice is used infrequently and has some limitations. A call can be sold at a higher strike than the long call covering it, and a put can be sold at a lower strike than the long put covering it.

Next-month calls can be sold at a lower strike than the long calls that cover them, but there will be a cash maintenance requirement of $100 per contract for each dollar difference in the strike prices of the long and short calls (and the same applies to puts in the other direction). The maintenance requirement is not a loan like a margin loan, and can be made in an IRA — it just means that a certain amount of cash must be left in the account and not invested in other stocks or options. In the *Terry's Tips* portfolios, we rarely incur maintenance

There is never just one cockroach.

— WARREN BUFFETT

requirements, and usually it is only for a day or two when we do use them.

When you buy (own) options at one strike and sell (are short) options at a different strike and each option is in a different expiration month, you have what is known as a diagonal spread. In order not to incur a margin requirement, the long option (the one you buy) must have a longer life than the short option (the one you sell).

Selling new options at a different strike than the long options that cover them (i.e., creating a diagonal spread) is a way to fine-tune a *Mighty Mesa* risk profile graph. More commonly, a more significant adjustment is called for. If, during the month, the stock has moved more than moderately in either direction, the portfolio might be close to approaching one of the shoulders of the mesa-shaped graph. If this is the case, rather than rolling over the current-month options to the next-month same-strike options (or to a different strike), the calendar spread should be closed. Instead of selling the next-month option, the long position already in place at that strike is sold.

The second roll-over Trading Rule (the 8% Rule) triggers the same action (taking off, selling, the calendar spread in question). When the strike price of a calendar spread becomes 8% higher or lower than the stock price, that spread should be sold.

The 8% Rule applies for underlyings that are not particularly volatile. If the implied volatility (IV) of the underlying is less than 30%, the 8% Rule is in effect. If IV grows over 30% and is under 40%, the trigger number for the Rule changes to 10%, and if IV exceeds 40%, the Rule number changes to 12%. For the past several years, both SPY and DIA had IVs which were well under 30%, but in the fall of 2008, they both grew to over 60%, so we did not trigger the 8% Rule until the stock price moved to more than 12% away from the strike price.

When a calendar spread is closed out because of either of these Trading Rules, cash will be generated. We will use that cash to move the shoulder of the risk profile graph further out in the direction that the stock has moved. For example, if the stock has gone up, and the current stock price has moved close to the upside shoulder of the risk

You're never a loser
until you quit trying.

— MIKE DITKA

profile graph, we would want to do one of two possible trades to push the shoulder to a higher level.

We could add a new calendar spread at a strike price which is higher than the current shoulder strike price, or we could add an upside butterfly spread. For only slightly more cash than the calendar spread would cost, we could add a custom butterfly spread which would involve a ratio of buying one call with a couple of months of life at the same strike as the upside shoulder strike, selling two current month calls at a higher strike (for SPY, we typically go 3–5 dollar increments higher), and buying one call at the same-increment-higher strike.

In the above example, this custom butterfly spread might look like this:

BTO 5 XYZ Jan-09 80 calls
STO 10 XYZ Dec-08 84 calls
BTO 5 XYZ Dec-08 88 calls for a debit of $1.50 —
(buying a custom butterfly)

Most of the time, the average daily decay calculation Trading Rule or the 8% Trading Rule does not get triggered, and the current-month options are rolled over to the next month same-strike options during expiration week. If the current-month short options are in the money, they absolutely must be bought back and replaced by the next month out same-strike options.

If the short options are out of the money, we have a choice of letting them expire worthless (and selling the next month same-strike options on the Monday following a Friday expiration) or buying back the soon-to-expire-worthless options on Friday and selling the next-month same-strike options on that same day.

We have learned that there is essentially no difference between the two choices from a financial standpoint. While buying back a soon-to-be-worthless option will cost a little (usually $.05 or less), the next-month option can generally be sold for at least $.05 more on Friday than it can on Monday (assuming the market stays flat, of course).

Take care to sell your horse before he dies.
The art of life is passing losses on.

— ROBERT FROST

This is true because two days of decay (over the weekend) takes place, and the options are worth slightly less on Monday.

At the award-winning brokerage where we trade (*thinkorswim*), there is no commission cost when you buy back a short option for $.05 or less. This feature tends to shift our preference toward making the trades on Friday rather than doing nothing and waiting until Monday (and this allows us to breathe a little easier late Friday afternoon when the stock sometimes makes wild fluctuations and what was once an out-of-the-money option suddenly becomes in the money).

During expiration week, every time a roll-over trade is executed, new cash is generated that is used to buy new calendar spreads. The strike prices of those spreads is determined by what we need to do to create a new mesa-shaped risk profile graph for the next month (with the current stock price just about in the middle of the B/E range of the mesa).

Generally, the new spreads are added at the end of the range that is in the direction that the stock has moved during the month. If the stock has moved up, spreads will be bought at higher strikes, and if it has moved lower, new calendar spreads will be bought at lower strike prices.

"Insurance" Adjustments

Other adjustments sometimes become necessary when the stock price moves more than moderately in one direction, and it becomes necessary to buy some "insurance" to protect against a further move in that same direction.

In our more conservative portfolios, we start out each month with some cash set aside (usually 5%–10%) to be used in case the stock moves sharply and insurance adjustments are needed (the actual adjustments are essentially the same as those mentioned above — new calendar spreads outside the current range of strikes in the direction that the stock has moved, or custom butterfly spreads).

If cash has not been set aside, the calendar spread which is furthest away from the stock price is sold, and the cash used for the most

To win . . . you've got to stay in the game.

— CLAUDE M. BRISTOL

appropriate form of insurance. (The custom butterfly spread provides somewhat better insurance against a big stock price move than the protection provided by a new calendar spread.)

In both cases, the key to deciding which adjustments are appropriate can be found by performing a what-if study on the risk profile graphing software or Analyze Tab at *thinkorswim*.

When to Close Out the Long Side

Our calendar spreads consist of owning (being long) options with several months of remaining life when the spread is originally purchased. At some point these long positions will need to be sold and the cash used to purchase new calendar spreads, perhaps at different strike prices.

In the past, *Terry's Tips* portfolios (which were carried out according to our *10K Strategy*) maintained long positions which were often LEAPS (with a year or so of remaining life). While LEAPS tied up far more cash than options with 2–5 months of remaining life, they provided additional protection against losses if the stock made a large move. Since they had such a long period of remaining life, they retained much of their value even if they were at strikes quite a distance from the stock price.

When we owned LEAPS, we needed Trading Rules to help decide when they would be sold and replaced with new and even longer-term options.

The *Mighty Mesa Strategy* does not use LEAPS for the long side. Instead, the long positions only have 2–5 months of remaining life when they are originally bought. Rather than depending on the long life of LEAPS to provide protection against a big stock move, we buy calendar spreads over a larger range of strikes than we did in the *10K Strategy* and use custom butterfly spreads on occasion. This policy provides the protection we need, and allows us to place a far greater number of spreads (which results in a higher potential return).

The long positions in the *Mighty Mesa Strategy* are usually maintained as long as possible (unless one of the adjustment Trading Rules

When I was young I thought that money
was the most important thing in life;
now that I am old I know that it is.

— OSCAR WILDE

is triggered and they are closed out early). If a February option is the long side of a calendar spread, when the January short side is near or at expiration and needs to be closed out, it will be bought back and the February option sold, and in doing so, the calendar spread disappears.

With the *Mighty Mesa Strategy*, we no longer need to worry about the proper time to take off a LEAP, since we never own them in the first place.

Additional Thoughts About Making Adjustments

In late 2008, I sent the following note to *Terry's Tips* subscribers. I apologize for using Greek terms that have not been introduced yet (but which are covered in Appendix A).

"Each day, I watch the net delta position of each portfolio and compare it to theta. If theta is higher than net delta, I know that the stock can move against us by a full dollar and we should enjoy a gain for that day. Of course, lately we would be happy if it only moved a dollar in a day — in the past that was considered to be a big move, but today it is a small one. If theta becomes less than net delta, I check out the portfolio on the Analyze Tab at *thinkorswim*, checking what will happen at the next expiration if the stock price were to move another 6%–10% in either direction (if expiration is only a week and a half away, I use the 6% numbers, and if it is more than two weeks away, I look at the 10% numbers). If a large loss appears imminent at one of those extremes, an adjustment would be in order.

As we know, adjustments are expensive. They invariably involve early rolling over (or taking off) spreads at a strike which is furthest away from the stock. That is the time when rolling over yields a very small amount and taking off involves selling for a lower price than any of the other spreads. It becomes even more costly when we add new spreads at the other end of the spectrum, usually at strikes which are closer to the stock price — these spreads are more expensive than the ones we sold. In the end, we are buying high and selling low, and incurring commissions all over the place.

Nothing will ever be attempted
if all possible objections must
first be overcome.

— SAMUEL JOHNSON

In a vacillating market, the best strategy is to avoid adjusting as much as possible to avoid these costs. As much as we would like to be delta neutral at all times, we would go broke making the necessary adjustments to make that possible. When the market makes a big move in one direction, the odds increase that the next move will be in the opposite direction. When a reversal move does occur, it would have been best to have avoided making an adjustment, and then reversing it later.

There will be months when the reversal does not take place during the month, and we will have to endure a loss for that month. Hopefully, we will gain it back in the next month when at least a partial reversal takes place.

That being said, adjustments are sometimes necessary to avoid a devastating loss in case the market continues to move in a single direction without reversing itself. When the risk profile graph shows that huge losses are imminent, an adjustment becomes necessary to ensure that we will still be around to play another day. It is hard to determine in advance exactly what mathematical parameters should dictate when this kind of adjustment needs to be made, and is often more of an intuitive decision.

The market has fallen by over 40% in one year. Retirement accounts have been decimated. Mutual funds are at lower levels than they have been for years. Everyone with stock market investments is suffering to one degree or another. But there have to be some good buys out there, and it is inevitable that at some point people will start edging back into the market. Who knows if it will happen this month or next, or the month after? But someday it should happen.

All it has to do is to stop dropping for us to make exceptional returns in our portfolios. Even though we get longer as the market falls (and get shorter as the market rises), there are times like today when we must tolerate being a little longer or shorter than we would like.

Our goal is to make as few adjustments as possible and still protect against a devastating loss of portfolio value. One way of doing this is

It isn't necessary to be rich and famous to be happy.
It's only necessary to be rich.

— ALAN ALDA

to establish, and keep, a wide range of strikes in our calendar spreads. We have already moved in that direction (especially in the *Big Dripper*), and will continue to do so.

As much as we would love to have hard-and-fast mathematical benchmarks for making adjustments, in this world of higher and higher volatility, it feels more like art than science, more intuition and less reason. It is an uncomfortable place to be for many of us, but that is the way it must be, at least right now."

Note: It is not always possible to follow the above Trading Rules precisely. Rather, they should be used as a guide for putting on and taking off positions. Short-term technical measures might cause you to deviate from these Trading Rules, or external downside events such as 9/11 would call for suspension of the 8% adjustment tactic (Rule 4) since the market almost always recovers fairly quickly from such events.

First get in, then get rich,
then get respectable.

— BERNIE ECCLESTONE

CHAPTER 12
Find the Right Discount Broker

If you want to trade options, you need to find an Internet-based discount broker who is options-friendly, has low commission rates, and allows option trading in your IRA. In addition, unless you want to deal with the hassle of placing all the orders yourself, the broker should have an Auto-Trade* system in place.

There are fewer than a dozen firms that meet the above requirements. I have checked them all out thoroughly. I worked with several of these firms for many years, and one of them eventually proved superior to the others on just about every possible dimension.

This Chicago brokerage firm goes by the unlikely name *thinkorswim*. You can find them at **http://www.thinkorswim.com.**

For a year and a half, (through *Terry's Tips*) I sent Trade Alerts (newsletter recommendations) to several brokers who had Auto-Trade programs. Then I discovered that *thinkorswim* consistently got better prices than any of the other brokers. Sometimes they saved my subscribers hundreds of dollars on a single trade.

I think there is a reason for their superior executions. Most online brokers place orders electronically through an automated ordering system. Unlike most on-line discount brokers, *thinkorswim* has an actual trade desk. Many of their brokers have over 20 years experience trading on the floor of the CBOE. For larger orders, such as the collective orders placed through Auto-Trade, a broker at *thinkorswim* telephones the orders directly to a specialist on the floor of an exchange (someone he probably knows personally), and often negotiates better prices than can be achieved on an electronic platform.

At *thinkorswim* you will find the best analytic software around and real-time stock and option quotes, all free. I also like their order entry

---

* Auto-Trade is a program where an investor signs a Limited Trading Authorization (LTA) with his or her broker which authorizes the broker to make trades in that account (with specific dollar limits) according to recommendations made by one or more of 50 or so newsletter publishers.

As they say in poker,
"If you've been in the game 30 minutes
and you don't know who the patsy is,
you're the patsy."

— WARREN BUFFETT

screen. You don't have to remember the option symbols to place an order, for example. That is a big benefit for me — I hate those gibberish symbols. Does ZYXCD really mean anything to you? And how easy would it be to enter ZXYCD and end up owning an option on a company you never heard of?

Even more important, you don't have to remember whether you are making an opening or closing trade — they keep track of it for you. Most online brokers make you figure it out for yourself, and even worse, they make you enter two separate trade orders if some of your trades are opening and another one is closing.

New option traders will find that they really hold your hand while explaining how to get started at *thinkorswim*. They offer great personal service (and no extra charges for telephone orders). They will get you set up for one of their Auto-Trade portfolios without your having to enter any orders. I don't know of another broker who offers this service.

You are offered a choice of commission plans at *thinkorswim* — their own, which has lower rates for very small orders, or you can select the same commission schedule offered by several other discount brokers.

There are a few other firms who have lower commission rates, but they have serious shortcomings as well. Most of them do not have Auto-Trade programs and more importantly, they do not have a good system for handling early exercise of short options that sometimes occurs. I have a collection of horror stories sent to me by my newsletter subscribers concerning some of these brokers.

Several brokers have asked me to participate in their Auto-Trade program by sending them my Trade Alerts as they are issued. (Of course, their clients would be *Terry's Tips* Premium Service subscribers.) While I understand that my business might expand considerably if I took them up on their offers, I have decided, at least at this point, to decline their invitations.

My reasons are two-fold — first, I am reluctant to expand my staff (we are a very small and skilled team that has been together for over

I walked home to save bus fare.
— Gee, you could have saved a lot more
by not taking a taxi.

— OLD JOKE

four years, with every member working from his or her own home here in Vermont). Second, I believe that *thinkorswim* offers the absolute best package of trading platforms, free analytic software, commission rates, and executions. I suspect that participating in other brokers' Auto-Trade programs would be considered to be a tacit endorsement of that brokerage, and I am unwilling to take that risk when I am convinced that *thinkorswim* offers the best available package.

I will continue to monitor other firms to see if their service improves to match that of *thinkorswim*, and let my newsletter subscribers know if another good alternative comes along. So far, it hasn't.

Discount Brokers and Trading Options in Your IRA

Unfortunately, many brokerage firms do not allow their customers to trade options in their IRA accounts. I believe they have this policy because they do not understand the options business, or if they do, they don't trust their customers to trade options responsibly.

Ironically, even if they understand that properly executed option trading can be less risky than owning stocks or mutual funds, most brokers prohibit such activity in IRA accounts. Fortunately, *thinkorswim* is not one of them.

Since I believe that the *Mighty Mesa* Strategy involves less risk than buying stock or mutual funds, I believe that trading stock options is a totally appropriate investment for your IRA. In October-November 2008, many mutual fund owners suffered 40% losses in their IRAs while option investors using the *Mighty Mesa Strategy* were smiling because their IRAs were worth more than ever.

In addition to the lower risk, there is one major financial reason to trade the *Mighty Mesa* in your IRA rather than a regular investment account — most of the profits are taxed as short-term capital gains. From a tax standpoint, it might as well be ordinary income.

Since most people think that stock options are risky investments, they can't fathom trading them in their IRAs. If you have read my arguments in this little book, maybe you can see that managing options

The highest form of ignorance
is when you reject something you
don't know anything about.

— WAYNE DYER

with a strategy such as the *Mighty Mesa* might be *less* risky than owning stock. After all, if the stock falls a little, you can still make money with this strategy while a falling stock will always result in a loss with a traditional stock purchase.

To change one's life: Start immediately.
Do it flamboyantly. No exceptions.

— WILLIAM JAMES

CHAPTER 13

Getting Started

I have tried to make the discussion of the *Mighty Mesa Strategy* as non-technical and simple as possible. It has not been easy. Trying to create options positions that never lose money is inherently a complex challenge.

I have tried to come up with precise Trading Rules that anyone could follow, especially in the area of making adjustments. But this proved to be impossible. Instead, I have set forth some general rules of thumb that can be acted up in conjunction with a close examination of the current risk profile graph for each portfolio. Depending on when during the expiration month (and the direction of the underlying price change), different adjustments might be called for. There are no hard and fast rules that can be applied in all situations. Even general rules of thumb can be misleading at times.

I think most readers will conclude that carrying out the *Mighty Mesa Strategy* is not a do-it-yourself project. It requires essentially daily attention, and most people have better things to do with their daylight hours.

The Auto-Trade Alternative

Fortunately, there is a method by which anyone can carry out the *Mighty Mesa Strategy* and have a life of his or her own. It is called Auto-Trade.

Auto-Trade is available at many discount brokers who specialize in options, including *thinkorswim*. In Auto-Trade, you authorize your broker to makes trades in your account based on Trade Alerts (recommendations to make a specific trade) made by any of 50 or so newsletters such as *Terry's Tips*. Before the broker will place trades for you, he contacts the newsletter and confirms that you are a paying subscriber to that newsletter.

*You can't expect to hit the jackpot if you
don't put a few nickels in the machine.*

— FLIP WILSON

There is no extra charge for trades made through Auto-Trade at *thinkorswim* (some brokers do charge extra, however). Since your orders are placed with many other investors as one huge order, the broker can often negotiate better prices on Auto-Trade orders than an individual can get through the automated options trading system.

Getting Set Up With *Terry's Tips*

There are four different ways for you to put the *Mighty Mesa Strategy* to work:

1) Do it on your own.
2) Subscribe to the *Terry's Tips* Basic Service.
3) Subscribe to the *Terry's Tips* Premium Service.
4) Subscribe to both the Basic and Premium Service.

1) Do it on your own. If you want to create your own *Mighty Mesa* portfolio on your own, without ongoing guidance from *Terry's Tips*, you know what you need to do to get set up with your broker. I hope I have given you sufficient instructions on how to manage the strategy. At first, you may want to use a service provided by many discount brokers (including *thinkorswim*) called paper trading – it allows you to try the strategy for awhile until you get more comfortable with it without risking any real money.

2) Subscribe to the *Terry's Tips* Basic Service. If you would like to mirror one or more of our *Mighty Mesa* portfolios with some ongoing guidance from *Terry's Tips*, our regular subscription service involves an initial purchase of our White Paper ($79.95). This report offers a detailed description of several strategies in addition to the *Mighty Mesa Strategy*.

The White Paper also includes a list of 20 "Lazy Way" companies where a 100% gain is mathematically guaranteed in two years if the stock stays flat, goes up by any amount, or falls less than 5% or 10%. Most of these stocks can fall by 25% or more over the two years and

A real decision is measured by the fact that you've taken a new action. If there's no action, you haven't truly decided.

—TONY ROBBINS

a profit is also realized. It is called the "Lazy Way" strategy because only two trades are made at the beginning of the period, and then you just sit and wait it out for an average of two years. (The "Lazy Way" strategy cannot be conducted in an IRA, but all the other *Terry's Tips'* portfolios can be mirrored in an IRA.)

Along with the White Paper, you will receive an Options Tutorial Program with a new lesson delivered each day for 14 days. In addition, you will receive two free months of *Insider* access. This includes our weekly reports which describe the current positions and risk profile graphs of several portfolios using several different ETFs as the underlyings.

After these two free months, you may wish to continue with our regular subscription program at the rate of $19.95 per month. The regular service includes Trade Alerts which are sent out at the end of the trading day for all the portfolios. These Trade Alerts include the specific trades which need to be made each portfolio and the prices that should be paid.

Since these alerts are sent out at the end of the day, the prices may or may not be available in the market on the next day. However, many *Terry's Tips* subscribers have successfully mirrored our portfolios with the regular subscription service.

To get set up with the regular *Terry's Tips* service, go to **www.TerrysTips.com/order/php** and check the box for the White Paper and Options Tutorial Program.

3) Subscribe to the *Terry's Tips* Premium Service. This alternative is designed for people who wish to have one or more *Mighty Mesa* portfolios managed in their own account for them through a broker's Auto-Trade program, or who need real-time notification of trades being made in *Terry's Tips* portfolios.

This is a simpler alternative. It does not involve buying the White Paper and learning all about trading options. Once you are set up with Auto-Trade, *thinkorswim* does everything for you automatically, and you can go about your everyday life without checking on the market every few hours.

*Don't be afraid to take a big step if one
is indicated. You can't cross a chasm
in two small jumps.*

—David Lloyd George

The Premium Service includes real-time Trade Alerts sent to you and your broker. This allows you to make trades at the actual prices that are available during the day when the alert is issued rather than waiting until the next day and hoping that those prices are still available.

The Premium Service costs $40.00 for the first month (which includes the set-up fee) and $49.98 for subsequent months unless you decide to upgrade your service and subscriber to multiple portfolios. This monthly fee is the same regardless of whether you have invested $5,000 or $1,000,000 or more. It is charged directly to your credit card and is not taken out of your broker account. (Of course, *Terry's Tips* has no access to or knowledge about your account. You are free to place other trades in this same account if you wish, as long as you leave as much cash that exists in the actual *Terry's Tips Mighty Mesa* portfolio account that you will see updated each week).

If you want to proceed with this alternative, your first task is to open an account (IRA or regular) at **www.thinkorswim.com**.

If you want to withdraw cash from your account as we do in the actual *Mighty Mesa* portfolios at *Terry's Tips* (see Withdrawal Rules in Appendix D), you will have to initiate this withdrawal on your own. *thinkorswim* makes it easy to do online.

To get set up for the Premium Service at *Terry's Tips*, go to **www. TerrysTips.com/order/php** and check the box for Premium Service and Auto-Trade. You do not have to do this until you have set up your brokerage account, but signing up early is a quick way to see exactly how the actual *Mighty Mesa* portfolios are doing, and give you some time to decide which portfolio is most appropriate for you to follow.

4) Subscribe to both the Basic and Premium Service. This $119.95 choice gives you all the instructional materials of the Basic Service (including the $79.95 White Paper) and two free months of the Premium Service (worth $99.96). This is the best choice if you want to learn everything we offer about options investing as well as actually investing some of your own money as well.

Just do it!

— NIKE AD

This ends my explanation of the *Mighty Mesa Strategy*. The rest of the book is for those who want to delve deeper into the details of the option world. It is not easy to explain any strategy involving options. They are derivative instruments which are complex and often confusing, and that is why very few people ever get involved with them.

In spite of the inherent complexity of options, I hope I have presented a relatively understandable explanation of why I believe this strategy has a high likelihood of achieving extraordinary investment gains year after year.

I invite you to participate in this adventure with me, and I wish both of us the best of luck on our journey together.

Part IV

$

APPENDIX
INFORMATION
for
DIE~HARD
STUDENTS

Time is money.

— Benjamin Franklin

Time is everything.

— Napoleon

I hate quotations.

— Ralph Waldo Emerson

The Greeks and Implied Volatility

The "Greeks" are measures designed to better understand how option prices change when the underlying stock changes in value and/or time passes by (and options decline in value).

My goal is to keep this discussion of Greek measures as simple as possible. It is not easy. I have tried many times to explain these terms to people in person. I have seen their eyes glaze over before I get past Alpha.

I'm sure you heard about the fellow who bragged that he could speak every language except Greek, and when asked to say something in a particular foreign language, answered "It's all Greek to me." Let's hope that isn't your answer next time you are asked about a Greek stock option measure.

I'll confine this discussion to three measures of market risk exposure — delta, gamma, and theta. Mathematicians gave these measures the names of Greek letters, or names that sound like they're Greek letters (vega, another measure which we will not discuss here, is not in the Greek alphabet, but sounds like it should be). Delta, gamma, and theta are the three most important Greeks in the world of stock options, and each tells us something important about an option.

If you own 100 shares of a company's stock, your market risk is easy to understand. If the stock rises (or falls) by $1.00, you gain (or lose) $100. It's not so simple with stock options. The most common way to measure market risk for an option is the Greek called delta.

Delta is the amount the option will change in value if the stock goes up by $1.00. If an option carries a delta of 70, and the stock goes up by $1.00, the price of the option will rise by $.70 ($70 since each option is worth 100 shares).

Owning an option which has a delta of 70 means that you own the equivalent of 70 shares of the company's stock.

All options do not have the same delta value. Deep in-the-money options have very high delta values (perhaps in the 90s), while way out-of-the-money options have very low delta values (could be under 10).

To make matters more confusing, delta values change over the life of the option, even if the price of the stock remains unchanged. An in-the-money option, which might have a delta value of 60 with a month to go until expiration, will have a delta value of essentially 100 on expiration Friday.

You can calculate the net delta value of your composite option positions by multiplying the delta value of your long options by the number of those options and subtracting the delta value of your short options multiplied by the number of those options. The resulting figure, net delta value, tells you how much the value of your current option portfolio will change if the underlying stock goes up by $1.00.

It is perhaps the best measure of market risk at any given moment.

Most professional market makers who hold a variety of options in their account, some long, some short, some puts and some calls, calculate their net delta value continually throughout the day so that they don't expose themselves to more risk than their comfort level allows. Ideally, they like to be net delta neutral, which means that with their current configuration of option holdings, they do not care whether the market goes up or down.

Gamma is a measure of how much delta changes with a dollar change in the price of the stock. This is a more complex measure, and really shouldn't be of too much concern to you as long as you stick with the calendar spreads like those used in the *Mighty Mesa Strategy*.

Just as with deltas, all gammas are different for different options. While you may establish a net delta neutral position (i.e., you don't care if the stock goes up or down), the gamma will most always move you away from delta neutrality as soon as the underlying stock changes in value.

If there is a lot of time left in an option (such as a LEAP), the gamma tends to be quite stable (i.e., low). This holds true for both in-the-money and out-of-the-money options. Short-term options, on the other hand, have widely fluctuating gammas, especially when the strike price of the option is very close to the stock price.

A perfectly neutral option strategy would have a zero net delta position and a zero net gamma position. As long as you deal with calendar spreads, you will never enjoy this luxury. You will always see your net delta position fall as the stock price rises, and watch your net delta position rise as the stock price falls. Gamma measures tend to do the same, which serves to accelerate the change in the net delta position of a calendar spread portfolio.

Occasionally checking out the net gamma position lets you know how big the change in your net delta position will be if the stock moves up or down in price. It helps you know how your exposure to market risk will change as the stock price changes.

Theta is my favorite Greek, because it tells me how much money I will make today if the price of the stock stays flat. Theta is the amount of daily decay. It is expressed as a negative number if you own an option (that is how much your option will decay in value in one day).

On the other hand, if you are short an option, theta is a positive number which shows how much you will earn while the option you sold to someone else goes down in value in one day. (The *Mighty Mesa* essentially always has a positive net theta position, meaning that time is on your side. It tells you exactly how many dollars you will make today if the stock stays flat. For me, knowing this number has some negative implications, however. If I'm at a restaurant on a night when the market didn't change much, I might remember the theta value that day — it was sort of "free" money I really didn't make any effort to earn. Oftentimes, I order a too expensive bottle of wine because of that silly theta number).

The ultimate goal of the *Mighty Mesa Strategy* is to maximize the net theta position in your account without letting the net delta value get so high or low that you will lose a lot of money if the stock moves against you.

This short discussion of the Greeks should be all you need to impress your friends next time you talk about the stock market. All you need to do is to get around to the topic of stock options, and drop a few Greek names on them (ask them if they know what their net delta position was yesterday, or did their theta increase much last week, and watch their eyes glaze over).

I have found that the Greeks are very effective conversation stoppers. Feel free to use them whenever the need arises.

Implied Volatility

Stock option prices are determined by a variety of factors. The most important are the stock price in relation to the strike price, the length of time until expiration, the interest rate (because an option saves you much of the investment required to purchase the stock), and the dividend of the stock. All of these factors are precisely measurable at any given point in time.

Yet if two different stocks have identical numbers for all of the above variables, their option prices may differ by a considerable amount. The reason is Implied Volatility (IV) of the option.

IV is the market's estimate of how much the price of the underlying stock will fluctuate in a year. It is expressed as a percentage. If an option has an IV of 30, this means the market expects the stock to fluctuate by 30% in either direction over the course of a year. IV is usually closely related to the historic volatility of the stock unless unusual events are expected for the company. (Historic volatility for all stocks which have options can be found at the www.cboe.com.)

IV is the best measure of whether option prices are "high" or "low." The higher the IV, the higher the option prices. This is true for both puts and calls.

An interesting feature of option prices is that IVs are sometimes different for different option months. IV for the current month's options tends to increase shortly before important company events such as the announcement of earnings or a rumored impending acquisition.

(IVs for longer-term options do not fluctuate as much when impor tant events are imminent.)

The *Mighty Mesa* does best if you can buy options with relatively low IVs and sell options with relatively high IVs. If you can find a spread where your long option has a lower IV than your short option, it clearly gives you a big edge.

I think there is a logical explanation for why the IVs for next-month options are often lower than any other option months — people are writing calls against their stock. Call-writers like rapid decay, and the next-month options provide the highest decay rates. If a large number of people are writing calls (or buying calendar spreads as the *Mighty Mesa Strategy* does), the prices of the short-term call options would become relatively depressed. In the case of calendar spreads, longer-term options are being purchased, pushing those option prices up (as well as their IVs).

For many companies, IVs do not escalate prior to an earnings announcement because earnings are relatively predictable. But for companies such as Apple (where quarterly earnings often fluctuate considerably) and Google (where company management doesn't tell analysts much about expected earnings), current-month option IV often skyrockets shortly before earnings announcements.

IV is an important factor in the success of the *Mighty Mesa*. Profits can be made with the strategy even if IV is not on your side, but you gain a huge advantage when you have it. When the IV for the short-term options (which the *Mighty Mesa* is short) is greater than the IV of the longer-term options (which the *Mighty Mesa* is long), we call this an IV Advantage. It allows you to buy relatively cheap options and sell relatively expensive options. While an IV Advantage is often difficult to find, it is worth looking for whenever you are considering a new company to trade using the *Mighty Mesa*.

Why Puts May Be Better Than Calls for Calendar Spreads

When you think of calls, you think about hoping the stock will go up. When you think of puts, you think about hoping the stock will go down. Those thoughts are appropriate when you are buying options. But they most certainly are wrong when you are buying calendar spreads.

When buying calendar spreads (also called time spreads), the strike price tells you which way you want the stock to go, not the choice of puts or calls. You always want the stock to move toward the strike price of your calendar spreads. That is where the maximum gain will take place, regardless of whether you own puts or calls.

There are two reasons why puts are a better choice than calls for calendar spreads:

1) The premium decay difference (the difference between the decay of the long-term options you own and the short-term options you have sold) is essentially the same for put and call spreads.
2) The put spreads cost less (usually in the neighborhood of 25% less) than the call spreads at the same strike price.

In the graphs on the next page, I have compared the risk profile of a typical calendar spread portfolio using calls and the same calendar spreads using puts. These spreads were set up for Sears Holdings (SHLD) at the 110, 120, and 130 strikes (at a time when SHLD was trading about $119). The long positions had seven months until expiration and the short positions had two months until expiration. Note the essentially identical curves. It truly does not matter whether you are trading in puts or calls from a payoff basis at each possible stock price.

Since puts and calls are opposites, our intuition would tell us that the options could not possibly achieve nearly identical returns if you used either puts or calls. But calendar spreads are entirely different from a strategy of only buying the options.

However, there is a major advantage to picking puts over calls. The 30 spreads in the above SHLD example would have cost $24,500 to buy with calls, and only $18,650 with puts. Both charts show a maximum profit of about $10,000 if the stock closes exactly at $120 on expiration, yet the put spreads cost 24% less to place, so the ROI for the puts would be 54% (at the maximum possible gain) compared to 41% if calls were used instead.

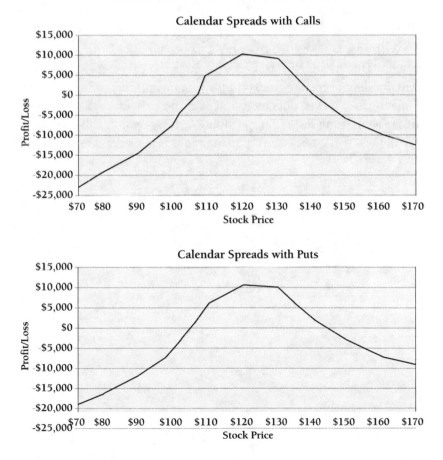

RISK PROFILE GRAPHS — TWO MONTHS OUT

When you buy calendar spreads, you should purchase them at the strike price where you think the stock is headed. If you are bullish about the stock, you buy calendar spreads at strike prices that are higher than the stock price. If you are bearish on a stock, you buy calendar spreads at strike prices that are lower than the stock price. In the *Mighty Mesa Strategy*, we buy calendar spreads that are above, below, and at the stock price to give us protection in both directions — we are not tied to the stock moving in only one direction.

Modification of the "puts are best" policy: For strike prices that are quite a bit higher than the stock price, it is better to buy call calendar spreads rather than put calendar spreads in spite of their higher cost. The reason is that the short-term puts are well in the money, and are quite costly. This high price means that they are not traded very actively. With inactively-traded options, a large bid-asked spread usually results. This means that you incur a large bid-asked-spread-penalty when rolling over soon-to-expire put options to the next month out. Sometimes, it is even difficult to roll over these options at a credit. For this reason, many *Terry's Tips* portfolios involve owning call spreads at the highest strike prices and put spreads at other strike prices.

A Note on Early Exercise of Short Options

S hould you worry about having your short options exercised? The short answer is "no." The long answer is also "no."

First-time option traders are often frightened by the specter of someone taking away their stock by exercising an in-the-money call. Many feel that they must maintain a large cash reserve to protect against such an event.

Many of these fears are based on their experience of owning stock and writing calls against the stock — early exercise results in their losing the stock (and incurring a taxable event if their original cost was lower).

In the option market, these fears are unfounded.

The holder of the option is almost always better off selling an option rather than exercising it. For example, if someone owns a soon-to-expire 80 call, and the price of the stock is $81, he could exercise his option and get the stock, making a $1 profit (less what he originally paid for the option, of course). Or he could sell the option for at least $1.50 or more, depending upon how much time there is until expiration. Right up to the last hour, there will be a time premium in that option that he would lose if he exercised rather than sold the option.

Only if you fall asleep or are lost without a phone in Antarctica will you have your stock taken from you when you don't want to.

At least this is true if you are trading options in liquid, (i.e., active) markets. In some inactive option markets, there are inefficiencies. The option market for an inactive stock may be entirely controlled by a single market-maker who is greedy, and not willing to pay a time premium close to expiration. In these markets, it may be necessary for an option holder to exercise to get the price he deserves.

What happens if you are exercised?

In the event that an exercise does take place, you should celebrate! You actually come out better than if you had to buy back the short option. Exercise eliminates the time premium you would have to pay. Your actual net cost is the intrinsic value of the option (the difference between the stock price and the strike price).

So what if you are employing the *Mighty Mesa Strategy* and you own a call with several months of remaining life rather than stock? In this case, your broker will sell (short) enough shares to satisfy the option-owner's desire to get the stock at the strike price. The very next day, you will have short stock in your account as well as the cash the option-exerciser paid to get those shares. You simply buy back the short stock, using the money that was paid to you when you sold it short.

Let's use an example. You have sold 10 July 80 call options short, and the stock is selling at $81 just before expiration. If you bought back these options, they would be selling at just above $1 — let's say $1.25 since there is still time premium in options up until expiration. It would cost you $1250 plus commissions to buy back the options.

If you get exercised, you sell the 1000 shares short for $80 each, or $80,000 less the commission ($15 or less at most discount brokers). You then buy back the 1000 shares in the market for $81, paying $81,000 plus commission. Your net cost was $1000 plus commissions rather than the $1250 plus commissions you would have paid if you had purchased back the options instead.

This works in an IRA as well, even though you are not technically allowed to short stock in an IRA. Your broker will insist that you buy back the short stock on the very next day, however.

Will I lose my LEAPS?

If you are lost in an African jungle on expiration Friday, and your short option is exercised because you do not buy back an in-the-money expiring call option, your broker will still not look to your LEAPS for payment. Instead, the proper number of shares of stock will be sold short in your account, and you will be asked to cover them (buy them back) on Monday.

If you are still lost in the jungle, your broker will buy the short shares back for you on the next trading day before ever considering a sale of your LEAPS (unless you have no other free cash in your account). **In short, your LEAPS are safe unless there are no cash or more liquid assets available for the broker to sell!** (This is exactly the same position you would be in if exercise had not taken place). Now that I have said this, I must qualify my statement by saying that *thinkorswim* would handle early exercise in this manner. I have heard horror stories from other brokerage firms where they indiscriminately liquidated other positions to cover an early exercise rather than buying back the stock with the cash sitting there. Your broker needs to be options-friendly and savvy.

One caveat. If you are short shares of stock, even for one day, and that day is the ex-dividend day (i.e., the day when owners of the stock are entitled to the dividend), you will be assessed the amount of the dividend. The only time this is likely to be any sort of problem is with the Dow Jones Industrial Average tracking stock (DIA), which pays a monthly dividend, and the ex-dividend date is on expiration Friday. The amount of the dividend is small, so it doesn't hurt much, but needs to be recognized. If you are short an in-the-money call on DIA during expiration week, it would probably be best to buy it back before Thursday.

For most stocks, a quarterly dividend is more common, and the ex-dividend date rarely coincides with the expiration date. Furthermore, on the day following an ex-dividend date, the stock usually falls by the amount of the dividend, so when you go to buy shares to cover your short stock, the price will be lower than it would have been before the dividend charge. **Once again, the net effect is about the same — whether you buy back the option or are exercised against.**

APPENDIX D
The Terry's Tips Track Record

This report is updated on the Monday following each monthly Friday expiration at **www.TerrysTips.com/TrackRecord**. Following is the report which was published on November 24, 2008.

Terry's Tips maintains several actual brokerage accounts where the *Mighty Mesa Strategy* is carried out with different underlying ETFs. Subscribers can follow every trade ever made in every portfolio. All results include full commissions paid at *thinkorswim's* default commission schedule.

For the second month in succession, the markets were down by huge margins unmatched in the history of the market. The average index fell about 15% in November. Over the last 10 years, in 90% of the months, SPY has fluctuated by less than double-digit amounts in a single expiration month. It has now fallen by double digit amounts for two consecutive months (24.9% in October and 14.7% this month, making a total of almost 40% over two months).

These percentage drops were the largest for the last 20 years. In the 9/11 disaster month, SPY fell by 14.1% (and quickly recovered the entire gain within two months).

Not only was the market down by huge amounts, volatility reached all-time highs. The *Mighty Mesa* strategy does best when the market is quiet. The last two months were periods of extreme high volatility. The most popular measure of volatility (VIX) hit an all-time high of 81% and ended up last Friday at 73% (in the past, anything over 30% was considered to be unusually high).

We figure that if our strategy could endure market melt-downs and volatility spikes like those that occurred in October and November 2008, we might really be on to something significant. So how did it turn out? We think we did pretty well. While the markets *fell* by 15% in the November expiration month, our composite portfolio total *gained* 14%.

Our *Mighty Stalagmite* (SPY) portfolio was set up with $10,000 on July 10, 2008. As our first portfolio that used the *Mighty Mesa Strategy*, it maintained a bullish bias so that the greatest gains would take place if the stock went up. Instead, from this start, SPY has fallen a whopping 36.4%. With volatility increasing so much and the stock falling by so much, our *Mighty Mesa Strategy* was severely tested.

However, in spite of all the bad things happening, the portfolio has gained 8.6% since it started. While this slightly lags behind our 36% annual goal, we believe that we have held our own through one of the most difficult times in market history without losing money.

The Special Situation in Russell 2000: While our composite portfolio value went up nicely in the November expiration month, the IWM portfolio incurred a large loss. IWM fell this month by 22.3% and 30.3% a month ago, making a total drop of 52.6% in two months. There is simply no way that our strategy can cope with this kind of volatility. It is little consolation that it has happened only once in 80 years.

IWM has higher option values (IV) than either SPY or DIA, so when markets do manage to be flat in a month, the IWM portfolio is expected to outperform the other portfolios. However, when IWM falls by an average of over 26% a month, we will surely lose money. It is a reminder that the best policy is probably to seek a little lower return and stick with the more conservative SPY and DIA portfolios.

***Rising Russell* (IWM):** This portfolio was set up with a bullish bias so that it would do best if the market went up. The 52.6% drop in IWM in October and November caused the portfolio value to fall 55% from its starting value 4½ months earlier. However, the current risk profile graph shows that the portfolio will recover this entire loss in the next two expiration months over a fairly wide range of possible stock prices.

***Oil Services* (OIH):** Since this ETF consists of only 18 companies in a single industry, it often fluctuates like a single volatile stock rather than an index. We consider it to be our most aggressive (least conservative) portfolio, and the huge drop in October proved just how risky it could be. OIH fell by a whopping 46%, and our strategy just could not cope with such volatility. OIH fell again in the November expiration month, but by a lesser amount (18%), and the portfolio made a nice gain that covered much of the October loss. In the 9 months of the portfolio's history it has lost 21% while OIH has fallen by 58%, but as in the other portfolios, there is a good chance that the loss will be recovered in the next month.

Durable Diamond **(DIA):** This portfolio was established four months ago and it took a big hit when the Dow fell by 23% in the October expiration month. However, when the Dow fell "only" 8% in the November expiration month, the portfolio gained enough to cover October's loss, and it is now up 23.6% for its existence, which works out to be about 70% annualized.

Mini-Diamond **(DIA):** In response to subscriber demand for a portfolio with a smaller cash requirement ($5000), we created this account in early December 2008. It is too early at this point to report gains or losses.

New *Big Bear Mesa:* This new $10,000 portfolio was established on September 25, 2008 and is designed to make money if the stock (SPY) stays flat or goes down moderately. It was set up to complement the other portfolios that do best if the stock stays flat or goes up. (While we try to start out each expiration month in a neutral net delta condition, our portfolios tend to have a bullish bias because the market does indeed go up more months than it goes down, in spite of last month's record.) Most subscribers seem to have other stock and mutual fund investments that only prosper when markets go higher, so the *Big Bear Mesa* portfolio should be an excellent diversification measure for them.

In its first two months of the *Big Bear Mesa's* existence, the stock fell by almost 40%. That is quite a bit more than "moderate." We were set up to handle a 10% monthly drop in stock price, but when it fell by double that amount, we had to scramble with many downside adjustments. However, over the two months, the portfolio managed to gain 24.1% in value after commissions which works out to be about 144% annualized.

Our "Most Conservative" Portfolio – the *Big Dripper*: In response the subscriber requests, we set up a new $10,000 portfolio (using SPY) on October 23, 2008 with an annual goal of about half our other portfolios but which would be as conservative as we could comfortably get — the portfolio could endure a 15% monthly swing of the stock price in either direction and still make a small gain. About 10% of portfolio value was set aside to make an adjustment if it became necessary because the stock fluctuated more than 10%. (Until October and November 2008, 15% swings in SPY had not happened in over 20 years, including the 9/11 terrorist attack market meltdown).

An important feature of the *Big Dripper* portfolio is that we will withdraw $150 in cash every month, regardless of whether the portfolio gains that much or not. If a "windfall" gain results, more would be withdrawn. If a retired person invested in 10 units of this portfolio (investing $100,000), he would enjoy an annual cash flow of $18,000 forever if the strategy works out the way it is supposed to.

We only have one month of results to report, but they are encouraging. The stock fell 15%, which was the break-even number when we set it up. During the month, we used the spare cash to buy some additional downside protection as the stock fell.

At the end of the first month in business, this "most conservative" portfolio had gained $1,758 in value after commissions. We withdrew the normal $150, plus an additional $1500 in "windfall gains" so that new subscribers could follow the portfolio with about a $10,000 investment per unit. In the very first month in business, this portfolio had gained almost what we expected to make for an entire year (it missed the mark by $43).

Summary and Learning Experiences: To best cope with huge market melt-downs like we saw in the October and November 2008 expiration months (and will probably never be duplicated again in our lifetimes), it is best to stick with the most broad-based indexes (DIA and SPY) which held up much better than IWM (considered to be the small-cap company index) and the most risky of all our portfolio offerings (OIH).

You can see every position and every trade we made in each of these portfolios by becoming a *Terry's Tips* Insider at **https://www. terrytips.com/amember/tt_signup.php**

Cash Withdrawal Policy: For all of our portfolios, the goal is to maintain the portfolios near their "starting" values so that new subscribers can mirror the portfolio at nearly the same initial cost. The "starting" values are $10,000 for all the portfolios except *Mini-Diamond* ($5,000). Cash withdrawals will be made from portfolios in increments of 3% of starting portfolio value. For example, for the 6 $10,000 portfolios, on the Monday following each monthly expiration, $300 will be taken out of the account if the account balance is over $10,300. If a gain of over $600 is made in a month and the portfolio balance is over $10,600, $600 will be removed that month. The goal is to remove $3600 from each $10,000 account over the course of a year (and $1800 from the *Mini-Diamond* since it started with $5000) and continue to maintain the original starting value of the portfolio.

Prior Years' Record: Before we made the big change in our investment strategy, our track record for the past two years was not so shabby either. From the beginning of 2005 until late in 2007, our portfolios had earned an average of over 50% each year. But when the market fell nearly 15% in a single expiration month ending in January 2008 (a drop equaled only once before in over 20 years), much of the 2007 gains were erased.

In January 2008, we dropped all our portfolios which were based on individual stocks (we had made over 100% on Apple options for two years running but lost nearly 80% when the stock dropped from $180 to $120 in a very short time). We also set our annual sights at the 36% target rather than a higher number, and created some portfolios that leaned to the bearish side for those subscribers who expected lower markets.

Many subscribers paired a bearish portfolio with a bullish portfolio using the same underlying as a way to hedge their investment bets.

For several months, the portfolios earned at better than the 36% annualized target, and then June 2008 saw another big drop in the markets. Our portfolios lost an average of 15%. The losses in the bullish portfolios were not enough to cover the gains in the bearish portfolios.

This unhappy experience made it clear that we had a strategy that made good money in most months but then gave up much or all of those gains when things went badly. We concluded that this was ultimately not a very sound long-term investment strategy.

On July 10, 2008, we amended our strategy to include exotic butterfly spreads to provide downside protection for the calendar spreads which had proved to be so profitable in most of the months, sacrificing some potential gains for the security of having a portfolio that might never go down in value.

A 10-year back-test of SPY monthly price changes showed that there was not a single consecutive 12-month period where the *Mighty Mesa Strategy* incurred a loss, and annual gains averaged 36% (over the 10 years, there was not a single month when SPY fell nearly as much as it did in October or November 2008, even in the 9/11 month when the terrorists attacks occurred).

The experience of our portfolios through the difficult months of October and November 2008 provided strong evidence that the 10-year back test results could be expected to be achieved in future months as well.

Please check our Track Record page frequently **(www.TerrysTips. com/trackRecord)**. It will be updated on Monday following each monthly Friday expiration.

The Shoot Strategy — an Options Strategy For Individual Stocks

In spite of the odds against winning, many people seem to like to invest in individual stocks – sort of like picking horses at the race track (and often for similar sound selection reasons, like the reputation of the trainer or the jockey or the color of his silks, or the horse's name or his recent race record, or what the touts are touting).

To my way of thinking, picking individual stocks is a whole lot more like gambling than carrying out a prudent option strategy such as the *Mighty Mesa Strategy*. But picking individual stocks is a whole lot easier and a whole lot more fun for many people.

If you insist on picking individual companies, the Shoot Strategy is a better way to make an investment than merely buying the stock. While it is not the *Mighty Mesa Strategy*, it uses the same basic idea — that the decay rate for LEAPS or other long-term options is much less than the decay rate of shorter-term options.

The strategy is outlined in my *White Paper* as the *Shoot for the Stars Strategy*. Les Brown said "Shoot for the moon. Even if you miss, you'll land among the stars. And Confucius said long ago "If you shoot for the stars and hit the moon, it's OK. But you've got to shoot for something. A lot of people don't even shoot."

So we call this the *Shoot Strategy*.

How the Shoot Strategy will perform:
- If the **stock goes up**, the Shoot Strategy will make money. The gain will be considerably greater than the percentage gain would have been if the stock had been bought instead of the LEAPS.
- If the **stock stays flat**, a small gain should result. Since you are collecting slightly more than the average monthly decay of the LEAPS each month (until they have only a few months of remaining life) you will make a small gain. However, even a small

gain is more than you would have made if you had bought the stock and it doesn't go up a penny.

- If the **stock falls**, a loss will usually result just like it would if you had bought the stock, and the loss will likely be a greater percentage loss than if the stock itself had been purchased instead. However, in many cases, the loss could be reduced (or eliminated) if the stock fell during those months when our Trading Rules call for selling in-the-money calls, or if more options were sold than was necessary to recoup the average monthly decay of the LEAPS (this tactic reduces the upside potential gain, however).

An example of the Shoot Strategy: In late October 2007, *Terry's Tips* used the **www.magicformulainvesting.com** to select 5 companies to demonstrate how the *Shoot Strategy* could work in the real world. We set up a separate demonstration trading account with $5000 for each company. One of the companies was *Accenture Ltd* (ACN) At the time, ACN was trading at $38.40.

We paid $7.70 ($770 plus a $1.50 commission) for each of the 7 LEAPS (Jan-10 40 calls). We calculated that the average monthly decay of our $5,400 worth of LEAPS was about $200 including commissions ($5,400/27 months = $200). Simultaneously with buying the 7 LEAPS, we sold 4 December 40 calls (which would expire worthless a month later) for $155 each, collecting $614 after commissions. Since we sold these calls as a spread at the same time we purchased the LEAPS, we only had to come up with the difference between our cost of $5,400 and our proceeds of $614, or $4,786.

The $614 we collected by selling the December 50 calls comfortably covered the $200 we would be losing for the two months of premium decay on our LEAPS. If the stock stayed absolutely flat for 27 months and we gained $307 each month, we would earn over 50% our money over that time span even though the stock had not gone up a penny (compare this result to what would have happened if we had purchased the stock instead — absolutely no gain would have been made).

Of course, you probably have figured out that if we sold 5 December 40 calls instead of only 4, we would earn a whole lot more each month. While that is true, if the stock went up strongly, we would not gain nearly as much as we would gain if we had sold only 4 short-term calls. Selling 5 calls instead of only 4 is more similar to the *Mighty Mesa Strategy* (where we are trying to maximize the amount of decay that we collect) than it is to the *Shoot Strategy* (where we are betting that the stock will go up and the majority of our gains will come from appreciation of the LEAPS we own).

If we had bought $5000 worth of ACN stock, we would have been able to get 130 shares. Our option positions were the equivalent to owning 248 shares of ACN, or almost twice as much as we could have bought with the same money.

Post-Note: Ten months after we started the ACN portfolio, the stock had edged up from $38.40 to $40.51. If we had purchased 130 shares with our $5,000 investment, we would have made a profit of $274 before commissions, or 5.5%.

This compares to a gain of $2,254 that we made in the ACN portfolio using the *Shoot Strategy* (after commissions), or 45.1% on the original $5000 starting value. The *Shoot Strategy* had worked exactly as it was designed. The stock edged up and our return was about 8 times higher than it would have been if we had purchased stock rather than traded the options.

We started 5 different portfolios in October 2007 using the *Shoot Strategy*, each using a different individual stock we had selected from the **www.magicformulainvesting.com** website. Over the next 10 months, the market in general was down considerably (the S & P 500 fell by over 10%). The average of our 5 stocks rose slightly more than 9% during this time span, providing a good test of using this website as a stock selection guide. (Two of the stocks fell in value while three rose.)

If we had bought the stock, we would have made a 9% gain for the time period. Our *Shoot Strategy* portfolios gained over 20% after commissions, more than double what would have made by merely buying the stock.

Every trade made in all 5 *Shoot Strategy* portfolios is available for Insiders at www.TerrysTips.com.

General Trading Rules for executing the *Shoot Strategy*:

1. Pick a stock you believe is headed higher (we suggest using www.magicformulainvesting.com as a guide — see discussion below).
2. Buy slightly in-the-money call LEAPS. At least two LEAPS must be purchased. If your budget does not warrant buying at least two true LEAPS, shorter-term calls can be purchased as long as they have at least six months of remaining life.
3. Calculate the average monthly decay of the LEAPS (time premium divided by the number of remaining months).
4. Sell enough slightly out-of-the-money current month calls to cover the average monthly decay.
5. A positive net delta must be maintained at all times (i.e., your total option position is long so that if the stock goes up, your investment will gain in value).
6. Near or at expiration, roll over the short calls to the next month (if they are in the money), again selling enough out-of-the-money contracts to cover the average monthly decay. If the expiring calls are out-of-the-money, let them expire worthless and sell the next month out, as above.
7. If short-term calls that have been sold become in the money (i.e., the stock has go up), they must be bought back during expiration week, and the amount paid must be added to the remaining decay of the LEAPS and a new (higher) average monthly decay bogey established based on the number of remaining months of the LEAPS.

There are a number of other Trading Rules that have proved to be successful for the *Shoot Strategy*, including how to change tactics if the stock should fall, how to adjust which calls to sell during seasonally positive (and negative) months of the year, and the best time to sell the original LEAPS. These important additional Trading Rules are included in the *White Paper* that is included in the *Terry's Tips Insider* service.

Deciding Which Companies to Buy: The best single source we have found for selecting individual companies is the Magic Formula system outlined in the small book by Joel Greenblat called *The Little Book That Beats the Market* and is available online at **www.magicformulainvesting.com**.

Rather than relying entirely on the Magic Formula, it might be even better to select individual stocks that also rank high at *Investors Business Daily* (IBD), *Value Line*, and by composite analyst rankings. In our opinion, using the *Shoot Strategy* offers considerably higher returns than merely buying the stock, and if you carry it out correctly, you can make money with the *Shoot Strategy* even if the stock falls in value.

Index

Dyer, Wayne, 168

E

Ecclestone, Bernie, 162
Education, 74, 82, 84
Eight percent Rule, 145, 149, 151, 161
Einstein, Albert, 5, 74, 92
Ellis, Charles, 19, 25, 29, 31, 32, 33
Emerging Markets ETF (EEM), 101
Emerson, Ralph Waldo, 48
Excel software, 125
Exercise of options, 79, 191
Exchange Traded Fund (ETF), 23, 95,
    97, 101, 103, 127, 194, 195
Ex-dividend date, 193
Expiration date, 69, 73, 87, 91
*Extraordinary Tennis for the Ordinary
    Tennis Player* (Ramo), 33

F

Flat markets, 11
Forbes, Malcolm, 86
Forbes Magazine, 116
Fortune Magazine, 26
Franklin, Benjamin, 182
Fridson, Martin S., 118
Friedman, Thomas, 11
Frost, Robert, 82, 152
Fuller, R. Buckminster, 84
Fuller, Thomas, 70
Full-service broker(s), 35, 63

G

Gamma, 184
Gandhi, Mohandas, 88
Gekko, Gordon, 72
George, David Lloyd, 176
Getty, J. Paul, 136
Google, 95, 97, 99, 187
Graphing software, 125
Greeks, 5, 157, 183-187
Greenblat, Joel, 204
Gross, William, 120

H

Half, Robert, 56
Harvard Business School, 41
Harvard Management Company, 29
Haskins, Ernest, 66
Historic volatility, 97, 186
Hopkins, Tom, 2
Hulbert, Mark, 11

I

Index fund, 27, 31
Implied Volatility (IV), 97, 149, 186,
    187, 196
Insurance, 75, 77, 91, 109, 111, 113,
    117, 119, 121, 153, 155
In-the-money option, 71, 153, 183, 191
Intrinsic value, 192
Investment advisor, 7, 45
Investment Illusions (Fridson), 118
Investors Business Daily (IBD), 204
IRA, 163, 167, 175, 192

J

James, William, 170
Johnson, Samuel, 158

K

Karlgaard, Rich, 11
Keller, Helen, 142
Kiyosaki, Robert, 28
K-Mart, 39

L

Las Vegas, 5, 31, 54, 77
"Lazy Way" strategy, 173, 175
LEAPS, 69, 155, 184, 192, 193,
    200-204
Leverage, 73
Lewis, Michael, 36
Limited trading authorization, 163
Little Book of Common Sense Investing
    (Bogle), 27
Long Term Capital Management, 95